THE
LEADERSHIP
WISDOM
OF
JESUS

THE
LEADERSHIP
WISDOM
OF
JESUS

PRACTICAL LESSONS
FOR TODAY

THIRD EDITION, REVISED AND EXPANDED

CHARLES C. MANZ

BK

Berrett–Koehler Publishers, Inc.
San Francisco
a BK Business book

Copyright © 2011 by Charles C. Manz

Berrett-Koehler Publishers, Inc.
235 Montgomery Street, Suite 650
San Francisco, CA 94104-2916
Tel: (415) 288-0260   Fax: (415) 362-2512   www.bkconnection.com

Ordering Information

Quantity sales. Special discounts are available on quantity purchases by corporations, associations, and others. For details, contact the "Special Sales Department" at the Berrett-Koehler address above.

Individual sales. Berrett-Koehler publications are available through most bookstores. They can also be ordered directly from Berrett-Koehler: Tel: (800) 929-2929; Fax: (802) 864-7626; www.bkconnection.com

Orders for college textbook/course adoption use. Please contact Berrett-Koehler: Tel: (800) 929-2929; Fax: (802) 864-7626.

Orders by U.S. trade bookstores and wholesalers. Please contact Ingram Publisher Services, Tel: (800) 509-4887; Fax: (800) 838-1149; E-mail: customer.service@ingrampublisherservices.com; or visit www.ingrampublisherservices.com/Ordering for details about electronic ordering.

Berrett-Koehler and the BK logo are registered trademarks of Berrett-Koehler Publishers, Inc.

Printed in the United States of America

Berrett-Koehler books are printed on long-lasting acid-free paper. When it is available, we choose paper that has been manufactured by environmentally responsible processes. These may include using trees grown in sustainable forests, incorporating recycled paper, minimizing chlorine in bleaching, or recycling the energy produced at the paper mill.

Library of Congress Cataloging-in-Publication Data

Manz, Charles C.
   The leadership wisdom of Jesus : practical lessons for today / Charles C. Manz. — 3rd ed., rev. and expanded.
      p. cm.
   Includes bibliographical references and index.
   ISBN 978-1-60994-004-1 (pbk. : alk. paper)
   1. Leadership—Religious aspects—Christianity.   2. Jesus Christ—Leadership.   I. Title.
BV4597.53.L43M36 2011
158'.4—dc22   2011009374

Third Edition
16 15 14 13 12 11   10 9 8 7 6 5 4 3 2 1

Interior design and composition by Detta Penna; adapted from a design by Beverly Butterfield. Proofreading by Katherine Lee; Index by Kirsten Kite.
Cover design: Susan Malikowski, DesignLeaf Studio

To all those brave persons who have
taken up the quest for a wiser and
more compassionate form of leadership
that seeks to unleash the inner
leadership and value of each person

CONTENTS

PREFACE TO THE THIRD EDITION

As I prepare this preface for the third edition of *The Leadership Wisdom of Jesus* I can't help reflecting on how much has changed since the book was first published. Issues of spirituality and religion in the workplace are no longer topics of questionable relevance for business and leadership practice. In fact, spirituality at work has become a widely considered topic for many business and management researchers and educators, as well as a significant concern for many executives and managers. When I wrote the first edition, this was not the case. In fact, writing the book as a business professor, consultant, and author was quite notable, and for many it was perceived as a rather bold undertaking, at the time.

Yes, many things have changed, yet paradoxically, many things have stayed largely the same. In fact, I believe much of what I wrote in the preface to the first edition still applies. Jesus taught timeless wisdom that transcends the ups and downs and ebbs and flows of years, decades, centuries and even millennia. Consequently, while the emergence of spirituality as a legitimate concern for the study and practice of leadership would seem to make this book even more relevant now as the third edition is released, the timeless wisdom it is based on has always been relevant, and I believe it always will be. Indeed, looking to the teachings of Jesus as a potential source of practical lessons for leading today remains a wise thing to do. Following is some of the original message I wrote in the Preface to the first edition:

> *The Leadership Wisdom of Jesus* is for those who want to become wise and highly effective leaders. It focuses on a uniquely constructive and compassionate approach

to leadership based on positive spiritual principles contained in the teachings of Jesus. It addresses priceless wisdom for leading ourselves and others.

When you are called on to lead, do you sometimes feel that you are hiding or suppressing your compassionate side as you struggle to function in the competitive business world? Do you find yourself projecting an image of rational control and competence simply to fit in and get ahead, despite misgivings about how your actions might be harming others or compromising your deeper personal values? Do you notice some dramatic contradictions between what is expected of you as a leader in serving your organization's bottom line and how you might act if you were simply behaving toward others in naturally humane and compassionate ways? Do you feel the need for an infusion of wisdom to help guide you to a more balanced and effective approach to living and leading that goes beyond your previous professional training and education? If any of these questions rings true for you, this book should provide you with some valuable insights.

The Leadership Wisdom of Jesus will appeal to those who are concerned with moral and humanitarian issues in work and human relationships. It draws on wisdom that blazes an effective leadership path consisting of such ingredients as compassion, humility, and service. It will also appeal to those who want to master a surprisingly effective and powerful way to provide positive influence for themselves and others. Its focus is consistent with important concepts such as soul, spirit, service, and servant leadership. It is especially relevant to managers, executives, and anyone in a position of influence or leadership.

Relatively few books on business, let alone business leadership, have drawn on the lessons of Jesus. *Jesus CEO: Using Ancient Wisdom for Visionary Leadership* by Laurie Beth Jones (Hyperion, 1995) is (a) prominent...exception. However, as its subtitle indicates, it focuses on visionary leadership, while the focus of this book is on empowering rather than visionary leadership. A visionary approach puts the spotlight on the leader's charisma and inspiration and tends to leave followers dependent and in the shadows. An empowering approach pulls followers to center stage and addresses how a leader facilitates and unleashes the gifts and abilities of others. This book focuses especially on interpersonal leadership prescriptions for empowering others that are suggested by the teachings of Jesus in the scriptures. It draws on those teachings to shed light on effective leadership of ourselves and others. The intent of this book is not to preach to or convert readers but to inform and equip aspiring leaders with the power of wise historical teachings that have dramatically changed the lives of millions.

I do indeed think many of these thoughts contained in the preface of the first edition still contain a relevant message for a lot of people, although there are quite a few more books on the subject now than there were then.

Then in the second edition I wrote a different preface. The following is part of the message it included:

When Berrett-Koehler approached me about preparing a second edition of this book, it triggered a flood of memories. The first edition of *The Leadership Wisdom of Jesus* was quite an adventure for me. Looking back, it was the publication of *The Leadership Wisdom of Jesus* that began my unexpected odyssey. I found myself on dozens of radio and television talk shows (often religious programs) explaining that I am not a minister or a theologian but rather a business professor and consultant who believes we have much to learn about leadership from the teachings of one of the greatest leaders that ever lived—Jesus.

Newspapers, magazines, and web sites provided further opportunities for me to share this message—compassion, forgiveness, and wisdom not only have a place in the complex, dynamic, contemporary, business world but can be a key part of realizing more meaningful, fulfilling, and even more successful careers and organizations. I also made many presentations at conferences, colleges, and churches. I encountered people in a variety of settings who had read the book and I heard about many discussion groups and classes using the book as a central resource. Ultimately, with a sense of humility, responsibility—and I must confess—surprise, I watched the book go on to become a bestseller.

The bottom line is that, despite (or perhaps because of) approaching the relevance of the teachings of Jesus from an organizational (as opposed to a religious) perspective, many people have found the book to be useful. My intention [in preparing this second edition] has been to preserve the general style, tone, and content that has been helpful to readers while adding some additional features that I hope will make the book even more useful. Specifically, I have added material that can serve as a discussion guide for reading groups and classes using the book. I have also added a new chapter that addresses perhaps the stickiest question that came up about the first edition—"How can Jesus' teachings about virtues such as compassion and forgiveness be reconciled with the realities of organizational pressures for things like profitability, efficiency, and accountability?" Further, I have gently attempted to update strategic places in the text and to add some additional examples that further bring the ideas in the book to life for living, working, and leading today.

Writing the first edition of this book challenged me to think more deeply than I ever had about what Jesus taught and modeled, and the character of his leadership. In reality, I had undertaken a journey toward personal development that would permanently change my career and life. Since then I have continued to spend a great deal of my time focusing on what has become a prominent topic in the organizational literature—spirituality in the workplace. I co-authored another book with my colleagues Karen Manz, Bob Marx, and Chris Neck titled *The Wisdom of Solomon at Work* and have collaborated with them, and with our friend and colleague Judi Neal, on several articles. The idea of living as a whole person, with personal values and beliefs, at work as well as at home has created a revolution of sorts and we have been a part of it. Most of the work in this area is careful to avoid dividing people based on specific religious beliefs (and in fact is often described as transcending religious dogma). At the same time it has provided a kind of permission for people more fully to embody in their careers the deeper beliefs that they live out with their families or in their places of worship. Consequently, it has infused their personal choices and behavior at work with virtues such as compassion and forgiveness despite their being in the "hard and competitive business world" that places much value on things like profit, efficiency, and control.

Now as I prepare this third edition, I find myself hoping once again that you will benefit from reading this book as I have from working on it and writing it. This new edition includes a new self-assessment chapter designed to encourage some personal reflection, several new examples, and some gentle updating throughout. Mostly, however, I remained true to my commitment to preserve the emphasis on Jesus' wise teachings and the insights they offer for healthy and effective self-leadership and leadership of others. Jesus had a way of getting to the heart of things that challenges us to think more deeply about the whats, whys, and hows of our lives and careers. His teachings have changed the lives of millions throughout history, and continue to do so today. To encounter them is to be launched on a journey toward deep personal change. And to lead with the guidance of these teachings is to become not only a wiser and more complete leader but to be more worthy of the mantle that leadership bestows on us when we find ourselves in any position of influence.

Finally, I want to thank several of my colleagues who have deeply affected my thinking about leadership, especially the compassionate aspects of effectively leading ourselves and others: Craig Pearce, Hank Sims, Chris Neck, Greg Stewart, Jim Mancuso, Bob Mitchell, Peter Hom, Frank Shipper, Bob Marx,

Judi Neal, and especially my wife, Karen Manz. I appreciate the valuable support and assistance I have received from my editor, Steven Piersanti, and from the very competent, wise, and compassionate staff at Berrett-Koehler. I also express my appreciation to all my other friends and colleagues who have supported my writings on leadership and teamwork over the years.

I appreciate the inspiration provided by such organizations as W. L. Gore & Associates, Herman Miller, AES, IDS Financial Services, Malden Mills, Semco, Dean's Beans, Equal Exchange, and many others, which have taken the quest for wise and compassionate leadership to heart. I am especially indebted to the wisdom provided by Jesus and the biblical writers, the teachings on which this book is based.

INTRODUCTION

A Call to Wise and Compassionate Leadership

When you are called upon to lead, in any capacity, are you effective? Is your leadership ethical and just? Are you able to provide positive influence for others that benefits them as well as the end that is being served?

Now let's go even deeper. Are you able to lead yourself effectively? Do you serve as an ethical, moral, effective example for others? Do you lead with humility? Do you lead with compassion? Have you mastered the arts of forgiveness and service? Can you be like a child when that is required? Do you understand and put into practice the Golden Rule? Do you know the secret of mustard seed power?

There is a powerful and informative literature dating back hundreds of years that addresses historical thinking on wisdom. It is especially centered on the writings and teachings of mostly ancient, and usually religious, leaders. A number of historical leaders and thinkers have achieved a special level of greatness and wisdom. King Solomon, Moses, Confucius, Lao Tzu, Buddha, Gandhi, Muhammad, and many others have struck a chord with multitudes in an unusually powerful way. As our contemporary knowledge continues to expand dramatically, it would be a grave mistake to forget the vast wisdom of such key historical figures.

It is in this spirit that I undertook this project. Initially I had intended to draw on the teachings of three or four renowned historical leaders, but I quickly concluded that the thinking of each deserves a separate volume. It is my sincere hope that reflecting on the leadership wisdom contained in this book will provide the reader with special insights that cannot be gained from contemporary leadership thought alone.

1

Of course times have changed over the past millennia. Some of us will question whether the wisdom of the ancient past is relevant today, especially wisdom that is often connected with religions. This is especially true if we take the traditional view of organizations as existing only to maximize profit and return on investment for shareholders. Yet looking beyond profit and financial return is quite a contemporary idea. Again and again companies that are putting the welfare of their employees and customers first are rising to the top as the highest performers over the long run. Sometimes an attitude of service is the best way to achieve bottom-line gains. But even when it is not, an enlightened and educated population is realizing that doing what is right (ethically, morally, and otherwise) is usually a much more satisfying and worthwhile way to live than focusing first on the bottom line. Besides, most of us could stand to learn more about wisdom, even if we choose not to act according to all of its teachings.

This book is about leadership lessons from the teachings of Jesus. The very name Jesus conjures up all kinds of images and emotions. Some people initially feel very positive and open. Others are hesitant. Still others are likely to be threatened and put off. My intention in exploring the leadership lessons contained in Jesus' teachings is to provide to a broad audience helpful insights that transcend cultural heritage or religious background. I sincerely believe that there is a great deal we all can learn about relating to and influencing one another from the challenging and penetrating teachings of Jesus. Indeed, his powerful leadership lessons point to a fresh approach that can enable both leaders and followers to maintain their integrity, live on a higher plane, and ultimately reach their personal and professional goals through sound, practical principles.

It is important to note that much of the wisdom of Jesus' teachings does not directly address leadership. Nevertheless, I believe that his teachings offer a wealth of ethical and practical guidance for leadership practice. Thus, throughout the book I will first share excerpts from Jesus' teachings, then offer reflections on the implications for leadership, and then suggest lessons for aspiring wise and compassionate leaders.

My intention is not to be religious in focus. Rather, I will address the subject of leadership in a way that captures some of the spiritual yet practical wisdom of the teachings of Jesus. Extensive debate has occurred on the literal veracity versus the symbolic nature of the Bible's account of Jesus' life and teachings. Some writers have questioned how many of the quotations found in the New Testament Gospels can accurately be attributed directly to Jesus.[1] This book will treat the biblical text as a historical record of lessons that are consistent with the tenor of Jesus' thinking and that provide wisdom from which to learn.

Jesus was especially fond of using parables—simple stories illustrating moral lessons—in his teaching. He also made extensive use of short sayings, especially aphorisms (memorable one-liners). Many of his teachings were repeated frequently, sometimes through a slightly different story or an alternative captivating saying. Although Jesus had a great deal to say about a variety of issues, many of his teachings focus especially on such common, powerful themes as the advantages of forgiveness over judgment, the importance of love and service, the power of humility, and the wisdom of recognizing the deeper value of every person. Consequently, some of the lessons I discuss overlap with others. This is arguably an important strength of Jesus' teachings.

He made sure that his important points were not missed. By reviewing important ideas, often from slightly different perspectives, his teachings were woven into a complementary whole. Ultimately, when Jesus' lessons have unfolded side by side, the complete picture they create might be thought of as a beautiful yet highly effective hand-painted fan, a priceless work of art for power-filled living. I hope that this book does a reasonable job of linking important parts of that whole to practical issues of leading ourselves and others.

Regardless of your religious beliefs, the lessons provided herein should help shed light on the path to effective leadership. More important, I believe, the lessons presented reveal a great deal about the constructive power of unleashing the positive spirit of leadership—of being right with the inner value and spirit of human beings—while engaging in the act of influencing ourselves and others. This is a very important goal because although many types of leadership can coerce, bribe, or inspire the desired behavior and performance of followers in the short run, long-run development and performance require influence that is more consistent with the inner truth of each person. I believe that all human beings desire (and perhaps require), at some level, dignity and a commitment to a positive spiritual connection with others. Treating people right and helping them to be right with themselves and the rest of the world is perhaps the only legitimate choice for long-term effective leadership.

One important caveat should be kept in mind: sometimes when we refer to positive personal outcomes we are talking about the very long term. Although Jesus addressed many practical issues and needs of his day, he was ultimately concerned with life beyond earthly existence. Thus his teachings were not necessarily intended to pay off in a human lifetime. Some of his wisdom may point the way to what is moral and good, yet not lead to the power, wealth, or other leadership trappings to which many aspire. In some cases, in the short run it may lead to the opposite. Surprisingly, however, Jesus' wise teachings are frequently proving to be consistent with many contemporary leadership principles that are leading to tremendous payoffs for enlightened leaders and their organizations in the here and now.

Many books have been written that prescribe leadership tactics designed to squeeze out immediate self-serving payoffs. Some instruct leaders to be commanding and intimidating. Others point to reward or incentive-based leadership that ex-changes desired rewards for follower compliance. Still others argue that leaders should be inspiring and visionary, swayers of the masses through charisma and the captivating pull of the leaders' causes. Leadership books have shared the insights of well-known military commanders, presidents, martyrs, and prominent business executives. Indeed, the lessons of a vast array of famous individuals have been written about at length, from Attila the Hun to Abraham Lincoln to Mahatma Gandhi to Winston Churchill to Lee Iacocca to Jack Welch. The lessons included in this book will draw from the wise yet practical insights of Jesus about leadership—a kind of leadership that is profoundly effective and at the same time based on a deeper wisdom and recognition of spirituality.

This book should encourage the reader to confront some very important but often overlooked aspects of being a leader. Bending the will of others to your own may serve your immediate objectives in the short run. However, the leadership that Jesus teaches offers some tremendous long-term advantages for the leader as well as the led. In the end, leadership based on sound, positive principles, such as living by the Golden Rule and leading by serving others, may be the only real way to serve yourself and master the true art of leadership. This art promises to ascend well above leadership myths that tempt us to become great in a worldly sense at the expense of other people. It teaches some seemingly strange but powerful leadership lessons, like racing for last place, cleansing your insides, putting the gavel away, and using the power of golden mustard seeds. These and many other lessons are discussed in detail in the chapters that follow. Careful study of these lessons may change your thinking about leadership forever and provide valuable insights into how to promote a more constructive and compassionate world for all of us.

PART ONE

CLEAN THE
MIRROR IMAGE

The first step to becoming an effective leader is to look in the mirror. Master the art of leading yourself and you will lay the foundation for helping others to do the same.

LOGS BEFORE SPECKS,
OR LEAD THYSELF FIRST

Why do you see the speck in your neighbor's eye but do not notice the log in your own eye? Or how can you say to your neighbor, "Let me take the speck out of your eye," while the log is in your own eye? You hypocrite, first take the log out of your own eye, and then you will see clearly to take the speck out of your neighbor's eye. (Matt. 7: 3–5; New Revised Standard Version)

As you consider the above passage, do some leaders you have worked for or people you have worked with come to mind?[1] Have you known some irritating hypocrites? This seems to be a common reaction, but perhaps the more important question is, did you consider yourself as one in possible need of the advice offered in the passage? If you did not, then perhaps this passage can be especially helpful to you.

Let's think for a minute. Would you like to become an effective leader? Would you like to have a significant and positive impact on others, on the world, or on history? Jesus provides some striking advice for moving toward this end. One of his key lessons suggests that if you want to lead others you should first—do what? Become more commanding so that you can bend the will of others to your own? No, that's not it. Work on your charisma so you can inspire others to do what you want? No, again. Develop the ability to identify what people want and provide it as an incentive for complying with what you lead them to do? No, that's not it either. Learn how to uncover the shortcomings of others and berate them for their failures until they do what you demand of them? No, no, no! All of these things may enable you to influence others, at least in the short run, but they just do not provide the proper foundation for effective leadership. The first step, Jesus seems to say, is to look in the mirror.

Usually when we think about leadership we think about one person (the leader) influencing someone else (the follower). In fact, when we are in a position of leadership it is typical to think that our job is to tell others what to do. That is, leaders are expected to evaluate others and tell them how they need to change and improve, and ultimately those others are expected to do what they're told.

Jesus' teachings, conversely, give rise to a quite different view of how we should approach the subject of leadership. We are challenged first to examine ourselves and get our own act together before we try to lead others. This is a hard lesson to learn. It is so tempting to want to skip this step. After all, pointing out the problems that other people have and providing the answers to their problems can be very gratifying; so can directing and commanding others at our whim. It can make us feel competent, special, and even superior.

"First take the log out of your own eye, and then you will see clearly to take the speck out of your neighbor's eye." This is a haunting phrase. It suggests that the very fact that we believe we know what is wrong with others, that we have the answer to their problems, and that we should direct them to our solution is a problem in itself. It is a log that can blind us to our own shortcomings. Jesus points out that we are focusing on

others' specks—relatively minor problems—rather than on our own large log, that we are ignoring our own log by presuming that we should direct and control others when we haven't even bothered to explore our own humanness and shortcomings. In that sense we are truly blinded by the gratifying feeling of power over others that enables us to forget how flawed, how messed up we ourselves are. Careful self-examination and a sincere willingness to seek ways of improving ourselves provide the foundation for effective leadership. When we don't engage in this honest self-evaluation and corrective process, we set ourselves up for doing more harm than good.

All this does not mean that it is never appropriate to try to influence—to lead—others. On the contrary, providing constructive, effective, ethical leadership is one of the greatest acts of service we can perform (more on leadership as service later). But leadership of others needs to come from an honest appreciation of our own humanness—from a sound, caring base of humility and a practical understanding of the unique human struggle that each of us faces as we try to be right with our life and the world. Jesus points to a kind of leadership that recognizes the value of each person and is exercised out of a sense of caring and commitment to the well-being of those being led. It also recognizes that each of us is ultimately our own leader when leadership is performed on a higher spiritual plane.

I have found this personal struggle to direct and motivate ourselves constructively to be at the heart of the search for a full and satisfactory life. In my own consulting and executive development work it has been humbling to realize that often things go much better the less I try to direct and "lead." Frequently my best work has resulted from simply listening sincerely and helping my clients figure out what is best for themselves—that is, helping and allowing them to solve their own problems. When I try to be wise and expert and force all my concepts, ideas, and knowledge into my service, I interfere with my clients' self-discovery. Worse, at times I completely miss the boat and get bogged down with my own opinions and view of the world.

I have learned that the best consultants are the ones who recognize how limited their knowledge really is, who continually learn and improve themselves, and most of all, who recognize that the real experts are usually the clients, who have to live with their problems every day. The trick is for the consultant to remove, or neutralize as much as possible, their own blinders (logs) and help clients sort through the often tiny specks that are blocking their own barely hidden solutions. I believe that the same principle applies to almost anyone leading or helping someone else: be humble and assume that most people know a heck of a lot more about their problem than you do.

By becoming more effective in our own self-leadership not only do we gain greater insight and empathy for others, who also struggle to make good choices and improve themselves, but we also serve as a model, which is central to leadership. Being a model in this sense does not mean that we want others to imitate and be exactly like us. Rather, we can serve as an example of someone who has sincerely struggled with being personally effective and has found his or her own way. As a result we are in a better position to help others find their own way as well. On occasion when I finish a training program or a consulting project the client says to me something like, "You really practice what you preach. You got us to solve our own problem." For me that is the greatest compliment I can receive as a consultant.

The powerful leadership lesson that Jesus teaches us is that if we don't take the important step of looking in the mirror and examining and leading ourselves first, we can be blinded by this shortcoming. It is as though we have a big wood sliver—indeed, a log—in our eye so that we cannot see others clearly. First remove the log and get right with yourself, then serve as an example and source of help (leadership) for others.

The primary prerequisites for leadership and for administering cardiopulmonary resuscitation (CPR) contain some insightful similarities. Obviously we need to be alive, conscious, and breathing before we start trying to revive others through CPR. Similarly, living and leading ourselves properly is like the breath that sustains our ability to lead others and to guide them on how to work and live. Many people believe that leadership is restricted to an outward influence process that requires leaders to lead and followers to follow, and that leadership is not something we can do for ourselves. On the contrary, leaders and followers form an organic whole that is required for leadership to unfold, and at the very core of the leadership process leaders and followers are one and the same. We can and do lead ourselves. Self-leadership is the breath, and without it the leader is in need of some serious leadership CPR.

That brings us back to Jesus' lesson of logs before specks. How can people expect to lead others effectively if they won't take the time—in fact, if they refuse to make an effort—to live their own lives (to lead themselves) positively and constructively first? According to Jesus they cannot. To do so is like trying to carry on without taking the time to breathe.

> TO BECOME AN EFFECTIVE LEADER FOR OTHERS,
>
> FIRST LEARN TO LEAD YOURSELF

THE LAST SHALL BE FIRST

He asked them, "What were you arguing about on the way?" But they were silent, for on the way they had argued with one another who was the greatest. He sat down, called the twelve, and said to them, "Whoever wants to be first must be last of all and servant of all." (Mark 9: 33–35)

Jesus took a surprising and fascinating approach to the topic of achieving fame and glory. In fact, he suggested that the only sure way to become great is to seek just the opposite. He taught that if you want to come in first, then purposely put yourself last. He directed that we should become last of all and the servant of all. That is an awfully hard pill for most of us to swallow. Much that we have learned about human nature suggests how important it is to build up our self-esteem and our belief in ourselves. In this spirit the virtues of accomplishment in athletics, academics, work, and so forth have been prescribed as healthy medicine for our psyche. The right to say, "I'm number one!" has become a compulsive quest for millions around the world.

Yet Jesus says, don't aim to be first; be last. What gives? I don't think Jesus is recommending that we should strive for mediocrity, or that we should waste rather than develop and apply our talents. Indeed, fruitfully using our gifts in constructive ways is a common theme throughout the Bible. But Jesus sends a clear message that we should not exaggerate our sense of superiority, that we should not become too caught up in our own importance. Most of all, he seems to be saying that those who are directly striving to be great as an end in itself are going at it the wrong way. Be humble and don't be a conceited self-advocate; be a servant and strive to put others first—this is the path to greatness, though often camouflaged and hard to see, that Jesus prescribes. Of course Jesus was especially concerned with greatness in a spiritual sense, in terms of God's realm, and not so much in a worldly sense. Nevertheless, the philosophy he advocated—humility, service, forgiveness—can lead to the kind of respect and love from others that many view as the real signs of "greatness."

Jesus went even further in his instructions to the disciples:

The disciples came to Jesus and asked, "Who is the greatest in the kingdom of heaven?" He called a child, whom he put among them, and said, "Truly I tell you, unless you change and become like children, you will never enter the kingdom of heaven. Whoever becomes humble like this child is the greatest in the kingdom of heaven." (Matt. 18: 1–4)

The idea of becoming like a child will likely affect readers in a variety of ways. Certainly the idea of becoming passive and naive will not strike many as particularly constructive. The important lesson that I take from this passage, however, is the idea of becoming "humble like this child." Again, this means resisting the temptation to become too full of ourselves, puffed up with an exaggerated sense of self-importance. Of course a variety of other positive images can be gleaned from mounting research that points to the positive benefits—increased health, creativity, ability to learn, and so on—of regaining some of our ability to be like children (playful, lighthearted, and inquisi-tive). Jesus' ideas run counter to many hardened adults' natural tendencies to become cynical, closed off, and self-centered in an increasingly complex and stressful world.

On another occasion, when Jesus attended what apparent-ly was a formal dinner at the home of an important man, he used the opportunity to teach further. This time he seemed to suggest that being recognized as important is not all bad, but it needs to be based on a solid foundation of humility.

When he noticed how the guests chose the places of honor, he told them a parable. "When you are invited by someone to a wedding banquet, do not sit down at the place of honor, in case someone more distinguished than you has been invited by your host; and the host who invited both of you may come and say to you, 'Give this person your place,' and then in disgrace you would start to take the lowest place. But when you are invited, go and sit down at the lowest place, so that when your host comes, he may say to you, 'Friend, move up higher'; then you will be honored in the presence of all who sit at the table with you. For all who exalt themselves will be humbled, and those who humble themselves will be exalted." (Luke 14: 7–11)

Most people appreciate those who don't emphasize their own accomplishments and status. This is especially true when that person does have the power or recognition to command the attention of others. We all want to feel OK about ourselves, and being around persons of some notoriety and power can provoke difficult emotional reactions. If they flaunt their status, we may feel inadequate or angry at their pretentious behav-ior. Conversely, if they act with humility and greet others with respect, we are able to enjoy their prestige and status. It is as though we share in it and experience it vicariously ourselves. Jesus' dinner story drives this lesson home vividly so that we are able to come face to face with the powerful correlation between humility and greatness.

When I reflect on these ideas I can't help but think of Donald Petersen, who led the Ford Motor Company at a crucial time in the organization's history. He became CEO in the wake of very high-profile leaders, including Henry Ford II and Lee Iacocca. It was difficult for many people to think of his name, and it was not unusual for newspapers to misspell it. As a leader he preached empowerment, teamwork, trust, cooperation, and the importance of every employee.[1] He openly confessed to enjoying his lack of star status. "We don't want stars. . . . Being part of a team is a much more productive environment. I feel very comfortable with the lack of spotlight and limelight."[2]

As an example of the positive leadership that Petersen brought to Ford, Jack Telnack, Ford's chief of design when Petersen was president, told the following story: After looking over a design, Petersen asked Telnack if the car depicted was the kind of car he would like to drive. Telnack pondered the question and decided to answer honestly: "Absolutely not. I wouldn't want that car parked in my driveway." Petersen then asked him to design something he would be proud of. The phenomenally successful rounded "jelly bean" cars (such as the Taurus) resulted. After years of autocratic leadership, Telnack's chance to do some self-leading had finally come at Ford, and he responded with one of the most successful designs in automotive history.[3]

This humble leader was indeed a key component of Ford's turnaround in the early to mid-1980s. And despite Petersen's low-profile style and avoidance of the spotlight, by focusing on others rather than on himself (his choice of humble seating), he was awarded a place of honor among leaders: in 1988, in a Fortune 500/CNN Moneyline poll, he was chosen by his peer CEOs as the most effective leader in America, even beating out the high-profile runner-up, Lee Iacocca, at Chrysler.[4]

More recently, it appears in many ways history has repeated itself. Alan Mulally, chosen as Ford's CEO in the wake of Bill Ford's relatively high-profile stint in the office, has demonstrated some similar tendencies to Petersen. Champion of the Boeing 777 airliner at Boeing, Inc., where he was discovered by Ford in 2006, Mulally came to the company with absolutely no car industry experience and is known to forgo tailored suits in favor of less grandiose khakis and blue blazers. Leading Ford's sale of the various more glamorous brands it had accumulated over the years—Jaguar, Land Rover, Aston Martin, Volvo, and Mazda—that distracted from its core business, Mulally helped orchestrate the return to a focus on the seemingly more humble (in comparison) Ford and Lincoln brands. Mulally became the sole American auto company CEO that turned down bailout money from the US government. Ford was the only company to avoid bankruptcy during the time that both General Motors and Chrysler failed, and more recently underwent a remarkable turnaround to profitability.

Mulally helped engineer a transition to encouraging getting along and working together collaboratively at Ford and less infighting between clashing fiefdoms headed by self-aggrandizing executives. He helped unite formerly competing factions where possible and, in some cases, helped those that couldn't work together to move on to somewhere other than Ford. His executive team was created largely from Ford veterans who would work together for a common purpose. According to Ford America's president, Mark Fields, a tipping-point event early in Mulally's tenure was particularly important for the then never-report-bad-news-or-else culture. [5] At a meeting of Ford senior global executives, Fields showed a chart with red on it, indicating problems with a new Ford vehicle about to be launched. Normally executives at Ford almost exclusively used green charts, as was the case at this particular meeting. In response to the unusual red chart, Fields said others in attendance slid their chairs away to distance themselves. The question was how would the new CEO Mulally respond? He applauded.

The message was quickly becoming clear. For Mulally, supporting one another and honestly admitting problems and mistakes that needed to be corrected was more important than feigning success to seek false adulation. And for this meeting, the man with the "last place" red chart, in comparison to all the other "everything-is-great" green ones, was symbolically moved to first position. Like Petersen, Mulally himself received acclaim for his no-pretense leadership—receiving the most reader votes for *Fortune's* Business Person of the Year in 2010 and being chosen as *Automobile Magazine's* 2010 Man of the Year. [6]

Overall, Jesus pointed to a fascinating paradox. Greatness comes more from avoiding it than from seeking it. Or maybe more accurately, the seeds of greatness derive from humility and service. Don't seek honor. Rather, let it seek you in its own way and when the time is right. Don't even think about it. Go about your business pursuing constructive work and focus on honoring and recognizing the contributions of others rather than your own. If you do this sincerely, your efforts will often receive the recognition they deserve, and more, as long as you don't seek and expect it.

I have personally found this to be true with many students I have worked with over the years. The more I have tried to honor my students and put them first, the more I have received honor as a result of their motivation and enthusiasm. When I have encouraged them to pursue their own interests and to apply and celebrate their unique talents, they have often pulled me into highly productive projects. Sometimes they seem to work too hard. On more than one occasion I have found myself advising "turned on" students to slow down a little, to work less hard on our projects, and in effect to honor me less.

In summary, try to rediscover natural childlike qualities (that are too often driven out of us at an early age) such as curiosity and playfulness that can feed creativity and innovation, and combine humility with a natural optimism that you can accomplish whatever you set out to do. All the while, practice being in awe of the unique and wonderful contributions each human being makes, and acknowledge and reinforce their efforts. These seem to be the lessons that Jesus wants us to learn.

Perhaps one of my favorite quotes, attributed to Nathaniel Hawthorne, sums it up best. It deals with happiness, but it could just as well have been focused on greatness. "Happiness is as a butterfly which, when pursued, is always beyond our grasp, but which, if you will sit down quietly, may alight upon you."

THE TRUE PATH TO GREAT LEADERSHIP

IS TO BE HUMBLE AND LOOK FOR

THE GREATNESS IN OTHERS

CLEANSE YOUR INSIDES

Do you not see that whatever goes into a person from outside cannot defile, since it enters not the heart but the stomach, and goes out into the sewer? It is what comes out of a person that defiles. For it is from within, from the human heart, that evil intentions come: fornication, theft, murder, adultery, avarice, wickedness, deceit, licentiousness, envy, slander, pride, folly. All these evil things come from within, and they defile a person. (Mark 7: 18–23)

In a modern age that places importance on the power of the image we project, Jesus' lesson offers a far different path to being personally effective. Books, magazines, TV shows, and self-help gurus have all pointed to the importance of impression management. We are directed to "dress for success," to use "power words," and in general to manage our external lives so as to impress and manipulate others in order to get what we want from them. We are encouraged to clean up our act on the outside, to create an external illusion of who we are, in order to get ahead in the world.

In contrast, Jesus says it is not the outside that counts. His words from the book of Mark specifically address traditional Jewish rituals concerning cleansing and purification related to eating, but he is really talking about much more. His real interest seems to be internal cleansing and purification—

developing qualities such as honesty and integrity. He is direct-ing us to cleanse our insides. In fact, he suggests that external things are relatively unimportant because they do not really en-ter our hearts. Instead, he challenges us, we should look within ourselves and get our internal act together.

It is hard to deny that many of us let ourselves go on the outside (which is a symptom of problems on the inside). Many of us eat or drink too much, and being a couch potato seems to be a valued art that countless persons are trying to perfect. Indeed, most us of us have a variety of external physical habits that need to be changed. But at least our extra pounds or our generally flabby appearance serve as a constant reminder and source of motivation to do something about it.

What is often forgotten is that we also develop poor men-tal habits, and consequently poor mental physiques. In fact, I would wager that most of us are in significantly worse condi-tion on the inside than on the outside. Excessive TV viewing, greater preoccupation with material things than with impor-tant interpersonal relationships, and a general avoidance of significant thinking and learning are all common symptoms of our poor internal condition. Other symptoms include self-serving, immoral, dehumanizing choices that flow from auto-matic behaviors driven by an excessive focus on the pursuit of ends such as power and profit. Consider the many leaders and organizations that in recent years succumbed to the tempta-tion to commit accounting fraud or other unethical business practices for short term gain (contributing to an array of dire outcomes such as a severe economic downturn, widespread unemployment, many hard-working people losing their life's savings, and countless families losing their homes). Enron, WorldCom, Tyco, multiple firms in the mortgage industry, and

Bernie Madoff's infamous Ponzi scheme, are just a few of the more dramatic examples that come to mind. Two thousand years ago Jesus sent a message that we need to heed every bit as much, perhaps even more, today—it's time to work on our insides.

Self-observation and self-analysis can be important foundations for internal self-cleansing. First, we need to take stock of our current internal condition. Observing and keeping track of thoughts that affect our general quality of life can be very helpful. For example, we can ask, What aspects of our work lives are we struggling with the most? What tends to set us off on a destructive mental tirade? We can even record our reactions systematically (when they occur, how long they last, what kind of dysfunctional behavior or physical symptoms result, and so on) on our smart phones or a slip of paper we carry with us.

Once we have made our observations, we can use the information we have gathered to analyze the situation. What can we do to create more functional responses? How can we establish new, more constructive mental habits? What sources of learning are available to us to address our internal deficiencies? Is there a good book available or a class we might take to begin the process of positive change? In general, how can we get our insides in better shape? What kind of mental, and perhaps spiritual, fitness program can we undertake?

For years I have assigned managers in my professional MBA classes and training programs personal self-leadership projects. They have tailored a variety of self-leadership strategies to address challenges in their own situations. A composite character, "Chris," provides an informative example based on recurring themes from dozens of these projects.

Chris suspected that his followers' and his own morale problems stemmed from occasions when his followers challenged his authority. For a two-week period he recorded notes each time he encountered a situation that caused him to be upset and to react in a destructively punitive way toward others. He discovered that he experienced an average of three or four of these episodes each day and approximately 90 percent involved occasions when his followers did not unquestioningly comply with his directions. As he reviewed the issues involved and the manner in which his employees had responded, he realized that he became upset when his orders were questioned or when the performance methods he prescribed were modified. In other words, unconsciously he had been resisting his followers' thinking for themselves and expressing their creativity, because of his insecurities about challenges to his authority.

Over the following months he consciously attempted to let go of projects once they were assigned to employees so they could have increasing freedom and psychological ownership of their work. His emotional and destructive reactions gradually diminished, and morale among his followers increased significantly. He concluded that the change had been difficult to make but well worth the effort. Most of all, he realized that his biggest interpersonal problems were the result of his own internal problems.

One of the reasons that cleaning up our insides is so important is that it can put us in a much better position to help others. This raises once more an important question we need to ask ourselves: how can we expect to lead others successfully if we cannot lead ourselves? The truth is, we usually can't. Inevitably our own internal conflicts will weigh us down and hold us back. Also, people nearly always see through the illusion that we have created. Our actions, behavior, and generally turbulent mental states will give us away.

Again, it cannot be emphasized too much that one of the primary ways that effective leaders influence others is through the example they set. Our choices and resulting behavior are usually more powerful and important than anything we say. And what is inside of us lays the foundation for what comes out of us. As Jesus said, *"It is what comes out of a person that defiles. For it is from within, from the human heart, that evil intentions come."* To demonstrate constructive behavior we must lay a solid foundation. Forcing ourselves to make a moral and/or compassionate choice in a specific challenging situation is not enough. Even if we manage to behave nobly this time, we may find it twice as hard to make constructive choices next time if our thinking has not changed in any significant way. If instead we place our effort on creating an efficient internal factory of effective moral thinking, we will establish a continuous productive stream of exemplary leader behaviors from which others can learn. Once we get our insides cleaned up, our outsides should take care of themselves.

OPTIMAL LEADERSHIP REQUIRES

THAT WE KEEP OUR INSIDES

(OUR SELF-LEADERSHIP HEART),

AS WELL AS OUR OUTSIDES, CLEAN

STOP WORRYING

Therefore I tell you, do not worry about your life, what you will eat or what you will drink, or about your body, what you will wear. Is not life more than food, and the body more than clothing? Look at the birds of the air; they neither sow nor reap nor gather into barns, and yet your heavenly father feeds them. Are you not of more value than they? And can any of you by worrying add a single hour to your span of life? And why do you worry about clothing? Consider the lilies of the field, how they grow; they neither toil nor spin, yet I tell you, even Solomon in all his glory was not clothed like one of these. . . . So do not worry about tomorrow, for tomorrow will bring worries of its own. Today's trouble is enough for today. (Matt. 6: 25–29, 34)

Do you make a habit of worry? Do you dedicate a great deal of attention and energy to worrying about failures of the past or concerns of the future? What is your honest appraisal of what you accomplish when you worry? What are the fruits of your worry labor? If the first step to becoming an effective leader of others is to become an effective self-leader, is being a persistent worrier the mark of a good leader?

Jesus articulated perhaps the most penetrating analysis of the futility of worry ever offered. His words in this regard are among his most poetic and poignant: "Look at the birds of the air; they neither sow nor reap nor gather into barns. . . . Consider the lilies of the field, how they grow; they neither toil nor spin, yet I tell you, even Solomon in all his glory was not clothed like one of these." Indeed, birds and flowers of the field don't scurry around driven by worry about yesterday's failures or tomorrow's potential disasters, and they do just fine. In fact, they do more than fine as they soar through the air and grace the earth with arguably life's greatest picture of beauty and most sumptuous fragrances. "Why worry?" Jesus asks. It just doesn't make sense.

Jesus' aesthetic piece of verbal art consisted of more than poetic prose based on nature, however. In fact, my favorite part of the worry-free philosophy he advocated deals with the issue of what worry accomplishes. "And can any of you by worrying add a single hour to your span of life?" In the book of Luke (12: 26) he adds, "If then you are not able to do so small a thing as that, why do you worry about the rest?" We are offered the penetrating challenge to reflect on what all the energy and time devoted to worry accomplishes. Obviously, unless we are masochistic, we do not enjoy the worry process for its own sake. As Jesus points out, it cannot add to our lives even a tiny instant in the course of time. In fact, the mounting medical evidence suggests the opposite: that the stress caused by worry can lead to a vast array of personal problems, including dramatically life-shortening illnesses such as cancer, heart disease, and many others. Indeed, worry cannot add even a tiny amount to our longevity, but it can significantly shorten it, and sometimes dramatically.

Stress from inner struggles and the multitude of pressures that require our attention at work and in our personal lives arguably causes more health and psychological difficulties than any other source. A plethora of studies have blamed stress for countless health problems and immense costs. Already before the advent of the current millennium stress had been labeled the "twentieth-century disease" by the International Labor Organization of the United Nations.[1] Today, estimates of the costs of work stress for the United States are in the billions each year as a result of healthcare expenses, lost productivity, and stress-related lawsuits.[2] Simply put, stress can make our lives a mess. And a very poisonous ingredient of destructive stress is the mental process we call worry.

Despite tremendous progress in knowledge and practice in health care over the past few decades, the epidemic of destructive worry and stress persists. For example, even before the recent recession, one of the major concerns of people at work was fear of job loss—a four-year survey of 2.2 million people found that nearly half of U.S. employees were worried about losing their jobs.[3] Further, nearly half believed that good work performance would not protect them from layoffs by the less loyal employers of recent times. Interestingly, this widespread worry was found at a time of relatively low unemployment. More recently, such fears are far more understandable as thousands of people actually did lose their jobs, pushing unemployment in the U.S. to nearly double digits. Add to that the vast increase of home foreclosures, loss by many of their life's savings in various corporate financial scandals, continuous technological advances that seem to require constant learning just to avoid becoming obsolete, a spate of natural disasters and terrorist attacks across the globe, and so on, and there really are some things that would seem to justify worry. Yet evidence and logic continue to expose worry as not only an exercise in futility but, in most cases, something that simply adds to whatever pain, suffering, and dysfunction we experience.

Of course, the fact that worry and stress can be quite harmful is not new to us; we've heard it all before. Furthermore, most of us accept and believe this persistent message. The problem is that doing something about the worry process is one of the most elusive challenges of human existence.

Worry can lead to physical drain, illness, psychological turmoil, and damage to interpersonal relationships. My own life has been replete with evidence of the destructive capacity of worry. In a previous career in retailing I had a boss who reported such extensive worry that he experienced persistent insomnia. He also developed a nervous stomach that frequently caused him to become physically ill. Another former coworker admitted that he drank heavily every night to deaden the pain of his anxiety and worry. Still another colleague was completely convinced that a close friend's death from cancer was caused by years of worry on the job. The cases are nearly endless. I have personally experienced depleted energy and various physical symptoms during stressful life experiences. So eliminating worry has become extremely important to me. Indeed, as noted earlier, evidence points to strong links between worry-induced stress and illness and disease, drug and alcohol abuse, and a host of the worst plagues of human existence.

Self-help books and seminars offering techniques that promise to remove fear and worry from our lives seem to be everywhere in our contemporary fast-paced, competitive society. Some of these books and seminars provide temporary relief, if not long-term benefits. Unfortunately, however, most of these potential remedies produce only short-term or inadequate improvements for most people. What seems to be needed is a more pervasive shift in our entire belief system and well-thought-out, customized behavioral strategies for addressing the all-too-seductive worry process. The real cure for worry may well rest in a fundamental shift in the way we view ourselves and the way we live on a daily basis.

I have personally found the philosophy and prescriptions of self-help psychology to be useful but never enough. So, like most people, I have continued my quest for the holy grail of peace and contentment that could provide a solid base for a healthy, power-filled life of personal effectiveness with as few worry-based, wasteful energy leaks as possible. In my broad search I have not found a more powerful yet straightforward philosophy than that offered some 2000 years ago by Jesus.

Jesus doesn't need contemporary research evidence to make his position convincing. Worry and the negative stress it causes detract dramatically from our enjoyment of everyday life and accomplish nothing of value. Worry occupies our minds with disturbing thoughts and causes our bodies significant pain. It makes us tired and ornery. And even though we would like to believe that it can be a sign of love for those about whom we worry, the drain it places on us actually makes us less capable of loving.

So what can we do about worry? Jesus suggests two important strategies. First, we can recognize our worry and its futility. That is, we can take charge of our thoughts rather than letting worry run wild to ravage our minds and our energy. Instead, we can become fully aware of it and recognize its wastefulness. This is an important first step because it can establish the basis, especially the motivation, for change. Second, Jesus urges us not to worry about tomorrow—to let today's trouble be enough for today. This exhortation is very consistent with the widespread conventional wisdom that calls us to focus on the present, to live in the moment.

Of course, many other prescriptions are available that build on the worry-busting philosophy that Jesus provided. For example, one approach based on a procedure described by Rowland Folensbee (the director of a Houston worry clinic) includes three primary steps: (1) recognize worry as soon as it occurs, (2) interrupt the worry with techniques such as progressive muscle relaxation or meditation (Jesus would suggest prayer), and (3) set aside a thirty-minute period each day to worry.[4] That's right, the final step calls for us to reduce our worry by confining it to an uninterrupted half-hour period each day. Instead of letting worry run unchecked, we are asked to save up our worries and then allow ourselves a controlled dose (not unlike an inoculation to fight disease) at a prescheduled time.

Many clients have experienced reductions in worry of nearly 50 percent using this procedure. For example, an insurance company president reported being a chronic worrier all his life. He was exhausted from sleepless nights, and his productivity and quality of life had suffered greatly. After applying the worry-reduction procedure for a few months, his worry had all but faded away. As he put it, "when I get into my worry session, half the time I can't even come up with something to worry about."[5]

In the light of all the logic—indeed, in the light of the unusual clarity of the folly of worry—Jesus seems to ask, so why not take charge of worry rather than let it take charge of you? Effectively managing worry may be one of the most self-empowering gifts you can give to yourself, and it can prove to be a significant step toward vastly improving your self-leadership and your ability to lead others to be empowered themselves.

TRANSCENDING WORRY CAN UNLEASH

THE VITALITY AND STRENGTH THAT LEADERS

NEED TO LEAD THEMSELVES AND OTHERS

COMMIT TO ETHICAL BEHAVIOR

*So they watched him and sent spies who pretended to be honest,
in order to trap him by what he said, so as to hand him over
to the jurisdiction and authority of the governor. So they asked
him, "Teacher, we know that you are right in what you say and
teach, and you show deference to no one, but teach the way of
God in accordance with truth. Is it lawful for us to pay taxes to
the emperor, or not?" But he perceived their craftiness and said to
them, "Show me a denarius. Whose head and whose title does it
bear?" They said, "The Emperor's." He said to them, "Then give
to the emperor the things that are the emperor's, and give to God
the things that are God's." And they were not able in the presence
of the people to trap him by what he said; and being amazed by
his answer, they became silent.* (Luke 20: 20–26)

Throughout the accounts of Jesus' life it is readily apparent that
he based his teaching on a strong moral and ethical foundation. Self-serving immoral behavior was just not an acceptable choice. This passage from the book of Luke describes a
fascinating situation in which Jesus is challenged to address an
emotionally charged, controversial issue. The question about
whether it was right for persons to be forced to pay taxes, particularly when many tax collectors collected more than they
were supposed to and pocketed a portion of what they collected, was a heated issue.

Given this situation and Jesus' assertive moral orientation, it was quite reasonable to expect that Jesus would answer that collecting taxes is wrong. In so doing he would be stating publicly his opposition to the authority of the state, potentially a very serious crime. But Jesus knew it was a trap. Further, he possessed an insight regarding the situation that was far more interesting than the simplistic response his challengers expected. In fact, he did not speak out against the collection of taxes at all. Instead he simply instructed that they should give to the emperor what was his and to God (Jesus' own moral foundation for what is ethical and right) what was God's.

Now, giving to the emperor that which is the emperor's is not a terribly original idea. We are faced with countless situations in which we are expected to give something to someone else that is rightfully theirs. When we purchase an item from a store or hire someone to perform a service, we owe them a payment that is rightfully due them. Even paying the government taxes to help pay for our nation's governance, for the services it provides and its other obligations, is a generally accepted obligation (though perhaps viewed by many only as a necessary evil).

The idea of giving to God what is God's, however, may be a bit more abstract and confusing. Perhaps a helpful way of thinking about this part of Jesus' message is to consider this as a call to do what is right—what Jesus might describe as God's will. That is, giving to God what is God's might be thought of as doing what is good and compassionate with the lives we have been given in light of how it affects others. From this perspective we are being challenged to serve "the emperor" (our organizations) to the extent that is morally and ethically right for them to expect. But this does not include stretching ethical limits into the realm of dishonesty or abuse of others.

In more than thirty years of studying leadership, I have en-countered and embraced many different views of what defines a person as an effective leader. One of these perspectives focus-es on exceptional persons who are able to create and articulate a captivating vision for others (followers) to pursue. Frequently this vision is communicated with considerable charisma and inspires followers to pursue a common purpose. Elsewhere I have used the term *visionary hero* to identify this kind of leader.[1] Interestingly, when I speak about this type of leader in refer-ence to historical accounts of the likes of Martin Luther King, Jr., Mahatma Gandhi, John F. Kennedy, or Joan of Arc, I gener-ally get a response of knowing understanding and admiration. However, when I mention the name of a visionary hero, like Adolf Hitler, I often receive a telling reaction from the audi-ence. People frequently have a hard time accepting such an an-tihero as a leader. Indeed, persons who wield influence with-out some minimally acceptable ethical and moral foundation are not considered fit by many to be called leaders. This call for a commitment to ethical behavior is in many ways at the heart of authentic leadership.

Unfortunately, the expectation that highly visible leaders will champion some level of ethics may not carry over into the interests, behaviors, or even leadership expectations of many ordinary people. In his book *Ethics in Practice: Managing the Moral Corporation,* Kenneth Andrews, former editor of the *Harvard Business Review,* pointed out how difficult it is to get business leaders to speak or write about business ethics. He described the difficulties in separating general ethical aspects of decisions from the specifics of the situation, and the hesitancy of leaders to speak out against even the most obvious unethi-cal choices made by others. This is largely true because they are acutely aware of their own vulnerability to close scrutiny (and even betrayal) when faced with highly sensitive, ethically loaded decisions. Their silence can suggest to many that they lack concern or give little importance to ethics.[2]

Professor Marianne Jennings, director of the Lincoln Center for Applied Ethics at Arizona State University, found some unpleasant surprises when she taught business ethics to MBA students.[3] Many of the students felt that studying ethics was a waste of time, and they resented it. Professor Jennings's student surveys revealed that two-thirds of these future leaders entered her class with shaky values and found ethical concepts to be quite foreign. "Some of them are pretty scary," she reported.

I find an interesting parallel here to the tendency of many people in organizations today to justify their own unethical behavior by rationalizing that the organization and its members are wrong in their actions. "Why not steal from the company when it is stealing from the public?" "Everyone uses company resources for personal use, so why shouldn't I?" "Besides, the company's profits are obscenely large and result from the exploitation of poor overworked employees like me"—so goes the logic. Thus, at one level Jesus refused to be trapped into advocating unethical behavior, even for the sake of what might be promoted as an ethical justification.

Author Keshavan Nair described how he has seen business executives shun colleagues who have fallen out of favor because they "lacked the courage to remain friends because they were afraid for their careers."[4] He contrasted this behavior with the moral courage of Mahatma Gandhi, who went against prevailing custom and power to work for the untouchables and advocated Indian independence in the face of existing law. When placed on trial for the latter action he stated to the presiding judge, "I am here therefore to invite and submit to the highest penalty that can be inflicted upon me for what in law is a deliberate crime and what appears to me to be the highest duty of a citizen."[5]

At times leadership calls for acts of moral courage. Aaron Feuerstein, whose story will be told in more detail in a later chapter, demonstrated this when his textile company was nearly destroyed by fire. He decided to risk his entire fortune to keep his employees on the payroll while he restructured the company, and all but saved the town of Lawrence, Massachusetts, in the process. Later he enjoyed substantial satisfaction from knowing he made a courageous moral choice, but as a side benefit he also enjoyed significant financial payoffs as well as a result.

It appears that Jesus may have been suggesting that money should not be a primary focus, even though he was confronted on a monetary issue. His greater concern in this lesson, giving to God what is God's, is not money. Perhaps he is indirectly saying that money is a human creation that, while it is quite functional, as often as not seems to produce more unethical immoral behavior than any good it produces. But as people like Feuerstein have found, ethical behavior can foster financial benefits.

And although some students have accused Professor Jennings of preaching Judeo-Christian values, she has argued that her curriculum is based more on simple financial math. She has attempted to show students that if they use shaky business practices, they will suffer. "Every time someone makes a poor value choice . . . there are severe consequences for the company, for the individual involved," she pointed out.[6] While the primary damage may be to personal integrity, among the negative outcomes she identified are loss of career and financial setbacks. Indeed, being ethical may prescribe less of a focus on money and more of a focus on honesty and the welfare of people, but the ultimate payoffs may well include financial ones.

In summary, Jesus says to give to the emperor what is the emperor's, but he does not direct that the emperor should be given the people's morality or dignity. Similarly, in our work lives we are challenged to give to our organizations only what is right for them to expect. It is not reasonable for our organizations to expect unethical or immoral acts from us. We should not be expected to deceive or cheat our customers or clients. We should not be expected to violate the law. We should not be expected to mistreat employees in order to squeeze out more productivity or cut costs. People should be treated with dignity and not as though they were unfeeling machines subject to the whims of a larger bureaucracy for which they work. Jesus' lesson suggests that we should give to our sources of authority that which is theirs to expect, but we should conduct ourselves with the moral dignity that is bestowed upon us as human beings. As leaders we are called to act with integrity and to expect no less from those we lead.

TRUE LEADERS ACT WITH INTEGRITY

AND EXPECT THEIR FOLLOWERS

TO DO THE SAME

LET YOUR LIGHT SHINE

You are the light of the world. A city built on a hill cannot be hid. No one after lighting a lamp puts it under the bushel basket, but on the lampstand, and it gives light to all in the house. In the same way, let your light shine before others.
(Matt. 5: 14–16)

The first section of this book has focused on lessons from Jesus that are primarily concerned with how we live our lives—how we lead ourselves. It is appropriate to close by addressing the lessons that others can learn from observing our example. In fact, the heart of leadership, in many cases, is the model that is provided by the leader. People pay a great deal of attention to what leaders do, how they live, and how they treat others.

This is a tremendous responsibility. Acting in shortsighted, self-serving, unethical ways will surely sabotage any attempt at positive leadership. Conversely, the visibility of leadership is a tremendous opportunity. We can project and amplify our positive leadership through our lives. We must walk our talk.

I personally have found this idea to be a constant challenge in my roles as college professor, as consultant, and perhaps most of all, as parent. When I extol the virtues of empowering others to my students and clients, I realize I must constantly strive to empower them. When I am asked questions that I know they need to answer (such as "What personal challenge should my class self-leadership project address?") I fight back my desire to provide the answer that my own ego and opinion urges me to proclaim and instead encourage them to decide for themselves. When I try to teach my kids moral principles and values, I am painfully conscious of my obligation to demonstrate ethical action in my own choices. When I am tempted to ignore the error the restaurant finally makes in my favor on my bill, I point out the mistake to the cashier and emphasize the importance of such honest choices to my kids.

We are indeed like lamps that need to be kept clean and cared for if we are to shine clearly and effectively. All of the other lessons in this section culminate in this powerful reality. Jesus challenges leaders to "let your light shine before others." He points out that we should not hide our example, and he implies that we should keep it constructive and healthy.

It is also important that we keep our actions consistent with our words—again, that we walk our talk. Jesus had the following to say about this issue:

> A man had two sons; he went to the first and said, "Son, go and work in the vineyard today." He answered, "I will not"; but later he changed his mind and went. The father went to the second and said the same; and he answered, "I go, Sir"; but he did not go. Which of the two did the will of the father? (Matt. 21: 28–31)

Clearly it is not enough to say the right words. We need to act on them and live them ourselves. To do otherwise is like deflecting and distorting a light. It is unclear where it is shining and what path it is lighting.

Of course one of the biggest problems with acting inconsistently with our words is that it creates distrust. How can people trust our message and positively respond to our leadership if they can't believe what we say? This idea is so basic and simple, yet so potent. Openness and honesty provide a solid foundation for leadership that enables others to give confidence and commitment to the leader.

CEO Dean Cycon provides a powerful example of a person authentically letting his light shine in business.[1] He founded Dean's Beans, a small specialty coffee roaster in western Massachusetts, in 1993. Formerly a lawyer and social activist, Cycon created the company as a vehicle for his social activism through business, a company that prioritizes social and environmental values over profit. All of Dean's Beans coffees are certified organic and Fair Trade, and harvesting and processing of the beans is done in conformity with international standards for the health of farmers and their environment.

Dean's Beans only purchases coffee from growers and importers that practice Fair Trade and that work towards better economic opportunity and improved health and nutrition in small farmer villages, largely made up of indigenous peoples who are trying to maintain their culture and lifestyles in a challenging world. Local empowerment and self-reliance are promoted through the firm's Fair Trade purchases and their work with local grassroots development and human rights groups. They also sponsor projects locally with disenfranchised communities such as Native Americans, the homeless and disabled, and many other groups trying to improve their lives and that of their communities.

Cycon speaks regularly about Fair Trade and corporate social responsibility to various business, social and educational groups and purposely serves as a living model of what he advocates. He describes how Dean's Beans operates so as to assure that every cup and every pound of coffee they sell contributes directly to the welfare of coffee growers and consumers. He explains how each player in their production and distribution cycle, from the farmer to the consumer, participates in socially just and environmentally responsible trade. He and his company serve as a shining example of virtuous business leadership and practice, and the hope is that other leaders and companies will follow their lead.

Another dramatic, and now classic, case illustrating these ideas was provided by the story of Ricardo Semler, CEO of the Brazilian equipment producer Semco. After experiencing significant stress and health problems, and after realizing that he had unmotivated employees due to his hard-driving disciplinarian leadership, Semler committed to an empowering style that brought out the self-leadership in others. First, he focused on getting his own act together: he reorganized himself before he reorganized his company. He slowed down and reduced his work hours. He cut back his eighteen-hour work days and began to let others experience commitment to and psychological ownership of the company. He completely changed his management style; empowerment and delegation became his leadership banners.

Semler espoused employee empowerment and took action to create it. He removed nine layers of management. He largely delegated his decision-making authority by letting workers do things like set their own hours, vote on all major company decisions, and in some cases even set their own salaries. Recognizing that status-conscious managers and existing hierarchy were the biggest obstacles to participatory management, he focused on getting managers out of the way of democratic decision making. Managers were not hired or promoted until all their future subordinates approved. Twice a year subordinates evaluated managers and all employees evaluated the company's credibility and top management.[2]

Semler's workforce trusted his leadership because he backed up his words with his behavior. Semler painted a striking picture when he described in his own words the environment provided for his workforce, which he held in high regard and viewed as being very responsible. "Employees can paint the walls any color they like. They can come to work whenever they decide. They can wear whatever clothing makes them comfortable. They can do whatever the hell they want. It's up to them to see the connection between productivity and profit and to act on it."[3] He let his own light shine as the central pillar of his leadership, and his company responded with performance (for example, a 600 percent increase in sales), loyalty, and trust. In the words of one of the workers, Semco "became a paradise to work in. Nobody wants to leave."[4]

As always, Jesus provides a formidable challenge. He says, *"You are the light of the world. . . . It gives light to all in the house."* And we are left with some questions that we need to answer: What kind of light will we provide? (Will it be moral and compassionate?) Who is in the house? (What people need us to light the way?) Where will the light lead from this time forward? (What kind of leadership will our lives demonstrate?) These are good questions for a leader to ponder. The primary lesson is that as leaders our light is always shining and it cannot be hidden under a basket. This lesson is true whether we choose to acknowledge it or not. Doing our best ostrich imitation by hiding our heads in the sand (or under a basket) does not make our leadership light go away.

Sometimes life provides learning opportunities through

some of the most unlikely sources. My family once had a very large cat. When in a playful mood she would sometimes initiate her own version of a game of hide and seek. She would approach one of us and then run to a chair or sofa and push her head underneath, apparently assuming that she was then well hidden. Her large furry body, with her sizable rear end dominating the scene, was in full comical view for all to see. Indeed, leaders cannot hide their choices and actions for long, if at all. They, too, tend only to display a rather large rear end when they try. The fact that a leader's light does shine for all to see is at once the tremendous opportunity and the burden of being a leader.

EFFECTIVE LEADERS LET THEIR LIGHT

SERVE AS A BEACON THAT LEADS

FOLLOWERS TO THEIR OWN BEST LIGHT

PART TWO

LEAD OTHERS WITH COMPASSION

Above all else, effective leadership requires compassion. When flawed human beings begin to lead other flawed human beings, compassion is the only dependable leadership ingredient that flows from real wisdom.

STONES UNDER GLASS

*The scribes and the Pharisees brought a woman who had
been caught in adultery; and making her stand before all of
them, they said to him, "Teacher, this woman was caught in
the very act of committing adultery. Now in the law Moses
commanded us to stone such women. Now what do you say?"
They said this to test him, so that they might have some charge
to bring against him. Jesus bent down and wrote with his
finger on the ground. When they kept on questioning him,
he straightened up and said to them, "Let anyone among you
who is without sin be the first to throw a stone at her." And
once again he bent down and wrote on the ground. When
they heard it, they went away, one by one, beginning with
the elders; and Jesus was left alone with the woman standing
before him. Jesus straightened up and said to her, "Woman,
where are they? Has no one condemned you?" She said,
"No one, sir." And Jesus said, "Neither do I condemn you."*
(John 11: 3–10)

This fascinating account consists of several interconnected com-
ponents that paint a challenging picture for aspiring leaders.
First, it makes it clear that there was no question about the oc-
currence of the condemned action: *"This woman was caught in
the very act."* So the offense is not in doubt; it happened. Second, the law of Moses commanded stoning such a woman. The

punishment was clear, but Jesus didn't buy it. Nevertheless, Jesus does not tell the people what to do. Instead he bends down and doodles on the ground in silence, leaving them to ponder the situation themselves. When they keep questioning him, instead of subjecting them to any proactive preaching, Jesus finally challenges them to examine themselves and make their own decision. He essentially says, "If you haven't sinned (made mistakes) yourself, then go ahead and stone her."

In this way Jesus empowers the scribes and Pharisees to lead themselves. No direct command or control is used. They are ready to condemn the woman legalistically without question. They pause only to use the situation to test Jesus, and he turns the tables by challenging them to think for themselves (to examine their judgment). As the people lead themselves away one by one, Jesus remains bent down, writing on the ground.

I have witnessed many good, empowering leaders facilitate the same kind of process, though perhaps less skillfully. The empowerment of employees is rarely helped much by solving problems and providing answers for them. They must learn to do this for themselves—that is, to be their own leaders.

In this passage Jesus challenges us to be at once compassionate with others and honest with ourselves. It may be embarrassing for us to admit, but it seems to be a natural human tendency to find in ourselves a sense of self-righteousness relative to the mistakes and failures of others. There is at least a little piece of all of us that is reassured when others seem more flawed than we are. Obviously this is one of the more negative features of being a human being and should be confronted and controlled to the best of our ability.

I believe that the lesson Jesus teaches goes much deeper than this, however. Often we can consciously or unconsciously contribute to the downfall of others. A primary way we do this is by condemning people for their imperfect humanness. This can be done with a verbal criticism, a withdrawal of support and loyalty when it is most needed—though perhaps least deserved—or even a small self-congratulatory smile for clearly having the upper hand at the moment. It is not enough simply to stay out of the public stoning of people who have stumbled. Jesus models an act of assertive compassion. He takes a stand to help others get back on their feet so that they can correct their mistakes, make amends, or at least keep stumbling along until they get it right.

Accepting and supporting others takes discipline and effort at times, especially when they have openly failed in some way. When a mob is gathered around for a public execution, it is hard not to get sucked into their frenzy. But Jesus leads us to look deeper, to search for the value and worth of every person, despite what they have done. This is not to say that consequences should not be suffered by those who have openly wronged others or been clearly unethical. But in many cases the obsession with accountability and punishment has been overdone.

I once had a wild limousine service van ride to an airport during a consulting trip. I hung on tightly as I was almost thrown from my seat several times while listening to the driver continually mumble about being late. Finally I asked him about his problem. I learned that his company's control system includes a three-day suspension without pay for being late for a pickup. The same penalty is assessed for an accident, regardless of who is to blame and how minor it is. As the driver attempted to make a left turn, he was forced to wait for some slow pedestrians. He shifted uncomfortably in his seat and explained that if he hit a pedestrian, "that's twelve penalty points, which is an automatic five-day suspension without pay." As I pressed hard with my foot on my imaginary passenger-side brake, I couldn't help feeling that the safety of the pedestrians might hang on the extra two-day penalty. While this example is a bit extreme, my experience and research have convinced me that organizations too often sacrifice employee commitment and customer service for employee control and compliance.

Conversely, sometimes failures are treated as positive learning experiences. The actions of a general manager of a small foundry owned by a large American automobile corporation is a case in point. He had recently implemented an orientation procedure to introduce new employees to the machinery they would operate. One day an employee reported to his office to explain a mistake he had made that had significantly damaged his machine and would result in extended and costly production downtime. His machine had malfunctioned during an unusually busy time in the plant, when no one was available to help him. In attempting to fix the problem on his own he had improperly grounded the electrical wiring, which resulted in the damage. The manager had personally gone over the proper procedure with the employee during orientation, but the employee had improperly performed an important step.

After explaining what had happened, the employee braced himself for the punishment he expected would surely follow. Instead the general manager simply asked if the employee understood why the problem had occurred and if he remembered going over the proper grounding procedure during the orientation. The employee answered yes to both questions and admitted he had forgotten and made a mistake. The general manager pointed out the safety reasons for the procedure and suggested that the employee go over the procedure again with a senior electrician.

The employee looked puzzled as he began to leave and stopped to ask, "Aren't you going to chew me out?"

The general manager responded, "No. I could do it if it would make you feel better, but I chew people out when they don't take initiative, not when they do. Do you plan on making the mistake again?"

"No way!" the employee responded emphatically. "Now I know what I did wrong, and I won't do that again!"

This general manager made a point of leading in a way that encouraged employee initiative, skill development, and self-leadership. Over time, with many similar leadership actions, he created a culture of effective employee self-leadership, and innovation and productivity continually increased while he was general manager.

Most people are hard on themselves when they screw up and don't need our help in inflicting punishment. And a very wide range of failures are simply the honest mistakes of imperfect human beings who are trying the best they can. Attacks and destructive behaviors that are leveled at others usually accomplish little more than driving them deeper into the self-destructive quicksand into which they have fallen.

Jesus challenges us to examine ourselves carefully. He leads us to the mirror once again for a sincere self-appraisal. A well-known saying warns that "people who live in glass houses shouldn't throw stones." The fact is, we all live in glass houses. They vary in thickness, but they are all glass nevertheless. The stones can quickly come flying our way when we encounter our many inevitable mistakes, screwups, and failures. Jesus said, *"Let anyone among you who is without sin be the first to throw a stone."* The passage goes on to say, *"When they heard it, they went away, one by one."* Probably one of the most difficult but kindest things we can do for ourselves and the world is to conduct such a penetrating self-examination regularly, especially when we are tempted to condemn someone else.

Some time ago I ran across an interesting tool to help with this process. It was a little stone glued to a piece of paper on which was printed Jesus' reminder that those who are without sin should throw the first stone. For a while I even carried the little stone in my pocket each day. I found myself reaching for it whenever I felt an attack of condemnation coming on. It would probably be a very helpful tool for all of us to keep such a stone handy, in our pocket or on our desk or wherever it would be obtrusive enough to serve as a healthy reminder.

Maybe we should all keep a centerpiece in a prominent location in our workplace (and home). I envision this centerpiece consisting of a beautiful serving plate or tray covered by an attractive sparkling dome of glass such as we might find at the finest restaurants. Under the glass would simply be a stone, perfect for throwing. A stone under glass: the perfect meal for the mind and spirit of an effective leader.

WISE LEADERS RECOGNIZE THAT

WE ALL LIVE IN GLASS HOUSES, AND

SUBSTITUTE COMPASSION FOR STONES

LOVE YOUR FRIENDS
AND YOUR ENEMIES

You have heard that it was said, "You shall love your neighbor and hate your enemy." But I say to you, love your enemies and pray for those who persecute you, so that you may be children of your father in heaven; for he makes his sun rise on the evil and on the good, and sends rain on the righteous and the unrighteous. For if you love those who love you, what reward do you have? Do not even the tax collectors do the same? And if you greet only your brothers and sisters, what more are you doing than others? (Matt. 5: 43–47)

Once again, Jesus' teaching poses a tremendous challenge. In addressing the centerpiece of his entire message—love—he teaches that we should offer this precious gift to everyone, even those we cannot imagine loving. Here Jesus is preaching a serious lesson about love that is in stark contrast to the frivolous way that love is frequently treated in our culture. Too often, love is viewed as an everyday commodity that can be bartered and consumed in our pursuit of wants and pleasures.

A kind of caricature of this idea is provided by a popular beer commercial from years ago that featured a man who apparently above all else wanted the advertised brand of beer. He tried a number of strategies to get what he wanted, but when all else failed he resorted to those ultimate words. He simply said, with much hyperbolic emotion, "I love you, man." Few commercials have struck such a positive chord with the public. I believe this reaction is due, at least in part, to our embarrassed recognition that love has become something we all too often withhold and use in exchange for receiving something in return. It was a funny commercial and a lot of its success was due to the comic nonverbal behavior of the beer-seeking actor. Nevertheless, the words he used are among the most powerful that any of us will ever hear—"I love you." Perhaps the use of those powerful words to weasel out of another person something as ordinary as a beer created such a striking contrast that it is hard not to laugh at the contradiction.

In this lesson, however, Jesus challenges us to embrace an even more dramatic contradiction. In fact, the contrast is so great that it moves well beyond the level of humor to that of the proverbial whack on the head with a two-by-four. He directs us to love not only our friends and neighbors but our enemies as well. Perhaps if he had used the word *tolerate*, or even told us to "like" our enemies, it wouldn't be so difficult to take in. But he says if we love only those who treat us well, we are no better than tax collectors (a group that in his day was at the bottom of the heap, and I'm sure that many will want to point out that they're not all that popular today either).

Why would Jesus instruct us to do something that seems so unnatural, that seems almost impossible to do sincerely? Some people might be able to force themselves, as an act of self-righteous sacrifice, to behave as though they cared about an enemy, but to really love a true enemy—that just seems like too much to expect. However, Jesus did offer some clues as to why this is such an important, though seemingly very odd goal to pursue. One piece of advice in particular sheds some light on the challenge of this lesson. He said,

> Come to terms quickly with your accuser while you are on the way to court with him, or your accuser may hand you over to the judge, and the judge to the guard, and you will be thrown into prison. Truly I tell you, you will never get out until you have paid the last penny. (Matt. 5: 25–26)

Ironically, following Jesus' prescriptions very often ends up benefiting us, even when they outwardly appear to be focused on benefiting others. In this case, he teaches that we should settle with our enemies so they won't attack us later—straightforward and sensible advice indeed.

A consultant colleague of mine learned this lesson while guiding an organization to change its warehouse operations from a traditional management structure to empowered work teams. Initially several middle managers felt threatened by the pending change and resented the consultant's input. One manager in particular became openly hostile. He believed that the new system threatened his standing in the company—that he could lose his job. Consequently, he vocally opposed the change and even confronted the consultant, claiming that the new work system would benefit only the consultant. When the change to teams was approved by upper management, the manager reacted by throwing his cigarette lighter across the room.

Clearly the consultant had reason to dislike this manager and even to hope that he would be dismissed from the company. But instead he tried to reassure the manager and communicate how the system could benefit him. He worked to insulate the manager from upper management and to ensure that the new system was approved without threatening his job. Eventually the hostile manager came around. He became a strong supporter of the new system and made several contributions to help the teams succeed. He was particularly instrumental in helping to develop a new language for the team managers' new roles as facilitators. He was awarded the nickname *Wordman* by his colleagues to acknowledge his contributions. He even publicly apologized to the consultant for his earlier behavior. He essentially changed from an enemy into a strong ally for the consultant.[1]

But there is much more to this lesson than a call to build better external relationships with difficult others. In fact, the realization that we often turn out to be our own worst enemy is a common experience that has contributed to conventional wisdom. If we focus on fighting, perhaps even hating, those who cause us problems, we create some very serious problems for our own health, well-being, and quality of life. Significant evidence has been found that supportive and loving relationships are very important for our mental and physical health. Even expressing and receiving affection from a pet can have significant benefits. Obviously, actively feuding with others is directly contradictory to the way this knowledge suggests we should behave for our own good. In addition, when we hold resentment toward others, in a very real sense we are more intimately bound to them than if we forgive and forget. Frustration and resentment will tend to fester as we resist letting go of wrongs that others have done to us in the past.

This does not imply that we should just continue to let others abuse us, but it does suggest that we should let the past go. Harboring resentment eats away at our insides and keeps us focused on the person whom we least want to focus on. We tend to be preoccupied with thoughts of how badly specific individuals have affected us. Consequently, those persons tend to become the center of our mental world. Ironically, the very persons whom we don't want to have anything to do with haunt us and become a greater focus than those we really do love and care about. In a sense we join our antagonizers in harming ourselves. Our negative thinking attacks us from the inside.

Conversely, by learning to love even those we consider to be our enemies, not only are we freed from being bound to the object of our inner frustration but we are also able to create yet one more source of positive support and joy in our lives. In essence, by expressing love toward our opponents, we create the conditions that may turn antagonists into colleagues. This, it would seem, is a powerful act of self-serving love. A major theme of this book is how we can empower others to lead themselves. By finding the patience and compassion to help difficult people grow in ways they are capable of, we end up serving ourselves as well as those we are helping to become empowered.

I have enjoyed the benefits of this wise approach many times in my life. At times I have been warned about new or current bosses, colleagues, subordinates, clients, or students. Other times, without having to be warned I have seen the cynical attitudes or difficult behavior of people with whom I have interacted. Nearly without exception I have found that if I resist the temptation to reject these people and withdraw from them and instead try to persist in my attempts to build positive, mutually supportive relationships, I am pleasantly surprised at the results. Many of my best relational experiences have resulted from working at building friendships and partnerships with people I have thought, or was told, were difficult. Now when I am warned to avoid someone, I become curious and hopeful; I wonder if it will turn out to be another opportunity to help someone else and myself to have a positive interpersonal experience. I also sincerely hope that others will do the same with me when I come across as difficult.

The world consists of all kinds of people. Some of these people are bound to clash with us—to have conflicting values, motives, and goals. Nevertheless, they are a real part of our world. I was once given the wise advice that we should seek out those people we dislike because they can reveal something about ourselves. That is, they may reflect, like a living mirror, some aspect of ourselves that we don't like or with which we are uncomfortable. As a consequence of this advice, in the spirit of learning I have sought out people I am uncomfortable with to engage in a meal or conversation. I have found this to be a very enlightening and worthwhile activity. More often than not I end up finding a lot to like about these persons.

By searching for common ground with the people we work and live with, we help to build a better life for ourselves in our jobs and personal lives. Similarly, if we help others to find themselves, to become less frustrated and more fulfilled in their own lives, they are likely to find the personal empowerment they need to become a better person. We may even discover that we have been more of an enemy to them than they have been to us.

Perhaps Jesus was trying to teach us that as we love others, especially those we least want to love, we are loving ourselves as well. And for leaders who sincerely want to influence positively all those with whom they come into contact, the idea of love is a powerful source of wisdom. Asking the question, is my leadership in this situation consistent with the ideal of expressing real love for the greatest benefit of those I lead? is perhaps the ultimate guide for effective leadership. This is especially true, it would seem, when we lead people we don't particularly like. Ultimately, the wise leadership to which this kind of thinking guides us is an act of compassionate self-leadership for our own benefit. Maybe the reason Will Rogers never met a man he didn't like is because he sincerely loved himself.

TRUE LEADERSHIP IS FOUNDED ON

EXPRESSING LOVE FOR THE GREATEST

BENEFIT OF ALL INVOLVED

THE GOLDEN RULE
AND BEYOND

In everything do to others as you would have them do to you. (Matt. 7:12)

The Golden Rule is probably the most powerful human relations strategy in the history of the world. And although it has been around for thousands of years and was prescribed by such spiritual leaders as Confucius and the Buddha well before Jesus prescribed it, it is still a sound principle today. Its practice can indeed produce valuable, golden results. The aim of treating people as we would like to be treated is to honor others as inherently valuable (spiritual) beings, as miraculous unique creations, no matter how seemingly imperfect and unworthy they are in their humanity. Each person is one of a kind; there are no duplicates.

Think for a moment about the ways you have been treated by various authority figures throughout your life. I suspect that you will recognize the simple fact that when you were treated disrespectfully, as an unworthy person of little value, not only did your view of yourself suffer but so did your view of the leader. The leaders for whom you were willing to go the extra mile were likely the ones that went an extra mile for you, the ones who believed in you even when you screwed up, the ones who recognized your great potential, your full value as a unique person.

Southwest Airlines co-founder, Chairman Emeritus, and former CEO, Herb Kelleher openly demonstrated a willingness to go the extra mile for Southwest employees during his leadership years with the company. He made it a priority to learn their names and to chip in and work alongside them when the situation demanded his help. He was observed lugging baggage and greeting customers in an Easter Bunny costume. He repeatedly demonstrated a truly exceptional level of caring and compassion for his employees, and his employees responded in kind. Perhaps the most dramatic example of their commitment to their beloved leader occurred when they pooled their own money and ran a $60,000 ad in *USA Today* recognizing him on Bosses Day. In the ad they thanked Kelleher for being a friend, not just a boss.

The way you treat others can become self-fulfilling. As a leader you will usually find what you look for in others; they will live up or down to your expectations. The Golden Rule challenges us to give others the same chance, the same respect that we wish to receive. A great deal of research has confirmed the power of the Pygmalion (self-fulfilling prophecy) effect. Perhaps the most famous of this research was conducted in the classroom by Harvard psychologists Robert Rosenthal and Lenore Jacobson.[1] They randomly labeled students as either bright or slow, based on fictitious IQ scores. When teachers were told which students were the brightest and the best (even though the designation was actually made randomly), the teachers treated the "special" students specially. They asked them more questions, waited longer for their answers, and generally paid more attention to these students. As a consequence these students actually became the better students—the special ones. Imagine what would happen if all students were treated as special? Imagine if we treated all of our followers and co-workers—in fact, everyone—as though they were special (which they are), just as we would like to be treated (because we're special too)?

At Herman Miller Inc., a highly successful and innovative manufacturer of business furniture (more on Herman Miller later in the chapter "Lead by Serving"), they go so far as to recognize everyone in the company as worthy of being a significant leader. Enabling and empowering others is central to the overall leadership approach and all members of the firm are expected to take the lead when circumstances call for it. This is called "roving leadership" at the company and involves taking responsibility and working in different capacities as part of serving the needs of the organization and its members. This means that all employees, to a significant degree, are treated the way most of us would like to be in our places of work—as important, even special, partners in the enterprise. Jesus did indeed advocate the Golden Rule, but he went even further. He suggested that we should treat people well, as we would like to be treated, even when they don't deserve it, and even when they act in ways that are harmful to us. He went so far as to suggest that if they attack us (strike us on the cheek) we should not fight back but allow them to attack (turn the other cheek). *"If anyone strikes you on the right cheek, turn the other also"* (Matt. 5: 39). This passive but powerful approach has withstood the test of time, resurfacing in dramatic passages of history, such as in the teaching of Mahatma Gandhi. His similar philosophy, many years later, resulted in a tremendous revolutionary shift of power that changed the shape of India forever.

In the end, Jesus went far beyond any normal interpretation of the Golden Rule. He sacrificed his very life for others—an act that is beyond our ordinary comprehension of what the Golden Rule means for our daily lives. Nevertheless, living and leading according to the Golden Rule at a more modest level offers us the potential to reap some very powerful results.

During a question-and-answer period that followed one of my leadership speeches, I heard a rather amazing true story that, although based on a mistake, follows in this same vein. A school administrator spoke up and shared from her personal experience. She had come up with the idea of sending a letter of commendation to the parents or guardian of any student in her school who had received at least three outstanding scores in conduct the previous semester. It sounded like a great idea to everyone present—that is, until she told us the rest of the story. It turns out that her assistant got the list of outstanding students mixed up with another list. By accident the assistant also picked up a list of students whose conduct was so bad that they were targeted for removal and placement in reform school. The letters were sent to the families of the students on both lists. What do you think happened? You guessed it. All of the students on the reform school list earned their way onto the outstanding list the next semester. For many of them this was the first time they had received so much attention, the first time they had been treated as though they were special. As a consequence they became special; they lived up to the treatment they had received.

The important lesson to learn from the story is not that we should reward people for behaving badly. It does suggest, however, that we should give others the benefit of the doubt, just as we would like it to be given to us, and more. A little empathy can go a long way. How would we feel if we were in the other person's shoes? How would we like to be treated? How should we respond to any situation when we follow the principle, *"In everything do to others as you would have them do to you"*? When you act according to this principle, you may well find that a powerful alchemy is unleashed in you and in the recipient of your actions. And the results can be even more valuable than gold.

THE GOLDEN RULE IS A

PRICELESS GUIDE FOR LEADERSHIP

PUT THE GAVEL AWAY

Do not judge, and you will not be judged; do not condemn, and you will not be condemned. Forgive, and you will be forgiven; give, and it will be given to you. A good measure, pressed down, shaken together, running over, will be put into your lap; for the measure you give will be the measure you get back. (Luke 6: 37–38)

Earlier we reviewed the story of the woman caught in adultery. When she was brought to Jesus as a test to see if he would condemn her, he simply challenged her accusers by saying that whoever among them was without sin should throw the first stone. Because none of them had lived a perfect life, none had never wronged someone else or made other mistakes, none of them met Jesus' criterion. As human beings it was impossible. So one by one they crept away.

In the passage introduced here, the message is carried even further. First a warning is provided. If we do not want to be judged, we should not judge others. If we do not want to be condemned, we should not condemn. This is a very important lesson that appears to be easily forgotten. When other people make mistakes, and especially when we must share some of the negative consequences, it is very easy to judge and condemn them. After all, their carelessness, poor judgment, bad motives, or whatever we believe caused them to screw up makes our critical attitude seem justified. Of course there is a high likelihood that we are misreading the situation, but in our minds we are likely to ask, Why shouldn't we judge and condemn them if they deserve it?

Jesus' simple answer is that if we do judge and condemn others, we too will be judged and condemned. I witnessed an example of this phenomenon when working with a large U.S. department store company; the essence of what occurred, with names changed for confidentiality, follows.

Bill, a new assistant buyer, was surprised at how judgmental and critical his boss, Tom, had been toward him in the first couple of months of his new job. It seemed that even when Bill did his job well, Tom found something to criticize. For example, when another employee left the company, Bill was assigned responsibility for the product area that this employee had been managing. When data came out showing that under Bill sales had improved by 70 percent over the previous year, instead of receiving praise he was vigorously chewed out because a small amount of inventory had been misplaced (it had been taken and used for advertising photographs without Bill's knowledge or permission).

When Bill and Tom met with the division manager to begin the annual department planning process, the tables were turned. The division manager was very critical of Tom and the way the department was being managed. At one point the harsh judgment and criticism continued unabated for five minutes.

Then, when Tom and Bill and the division manager reported to the group vice president for the next stage of the planning process, the pattern continued. The vice president was very critical of the division manager and the way the division was being managed. Ultimately he proclaimed that the president would tear the division manager apart when they met for the final stage of the annual planning process. Apparently he wasn't aware of Jesus' warning that you should not judge or you will be judged, but that's exactly what happened. At one point in the next meeting, the president was so harsh in his comments that Bill couldn't help feeling sorry and embarrassed for the vice president. "Didn't you tell them to address the impact of our new strategic plan on their departments?" the president barked. "How in the hell do you expect us to make a profit if you don't manage your people?"

The reality is that we are all flawed human beings. We may have our more noble, praiseworthy moments, but inevitably we will fall on our faces. Even when we seem to be getting our act together, we can depend on the fact that it won't last forever. Throughout my life, especially when I was a youth, I have struggled with the reality that even our most exemplary heroes have days when they become the dunce, the doofus. World-class athletes, exemplary politicians (there are some), outstanding teachers, philanthropists, inspirational speakers, religious leaders, and countless others have their bad days. Sometimes they have really bad days, but don't we all? The reality is that everyone—there are *no* exceptions to this—will let others down, will blow it some of the time. And when our turn comes you can bet that those with the greatest desire to lead the lynch mob will be the very ones we were condemning and ready to lynch when it was their turn. As the saying goes, what goes around comes around.

Sadly, many leaders have had to learn this lesson the hard way. Richard Snyder, former CEO of Simon & Schuster, is a case in point. His leadership was commonly described as a reign of fear and intimidation. When *Newsweek* interviewed his employees, they found he was "loathed as a boss." Words used to describe his leadership included *intimidation, fear, erratic, demanding,* and *imperious.* Reportedly he was prone to firing employees he rode with on an elevator. Many employees got the message and declined to enter an elevator with him; Snyder liked it that way. When Viacom acquired Paramount, the parent company of Simon & Schuster, Snyder ended up being fired by Frank Biondi Jr., president of Viacom, because of his leadership style and the impact it was having on his employees.[1] What goes around comes around indeed.

Another negative result that can be created by too much judging is that problems are driven underground. No one wants to be a messenger bearing bad news to a judgmental leader. Remember the limousine service van driver I talked about in the chapter "Stones Under Glass"? He was well aware of this problem. After describing his organization's punitive control system, he gave me a short lecture on the problems with American businesses. He pointed out, "The right hand doesn't know what the left hand is doing; management and workers don't work together. Often a problem will continue for weeks in U.S. companies because workers don't tell management about it. Why should they, if they think management is just out to screw them? They just kick us in the rear." This driver described a situation that is all too true for leaders and organizations that rely on judgment and punishment.

Indeed, with an atmosphere of judgment, the kind of information needed to address and fix problems does not come to the surface. In the chapter "The Last Shall be First," I talked about the culture at Ford prior to Alan Mulally becoming CEO, where managers avoided reporting bad news for fear of judgment and reprimand. I also shared a key example that is worth repeating again here. Around that time, the company was tee-

PUT THE GAVEL AWAY   75

tering on the brink of bankruptcy. This was a fate which key competitors GM and Chrysler eventually succumbed to but Ford, guided by Mulally's leadership, was able to avoid with a striking corporate turnaround. In a key meeting, when a Ford executive finally reported some problems with a new vehicle that needed to be addressed, rather than taking out the judgment gavel, Mulally congratulated him with applause. Later, the executive that reported the problem described this as a tipping-point event that helped save the company. Judgmental leadership drives underground the kind of truthfulness and honesty that is needed for learning and making improvements, allowing problems to fester and potentially turn into crises.

In addition, when we judge and condemn others, especially when we get particularly worked up and indignant, the negativity can eat away at us. To combat this kind of self-destructive process, Jon Kabat-Zinn founded and became director of the Stress Reduction Clinic at the University of Massachusetts Medical Center, which has done extensive work on the healthful benefits of practicing mindfulness meditation. An ancient Buddhist practice, mindfulness can be applied to help us wake up from automatic and unconscious living and enjoy a more healthy, fully conscious lifestyle.[2] An essential ingredient of this approach is to eliminate the constant tendency to judge everything and everyone, a practice that can dominate and weigh down the mind. Kabat-Zinn likens the tendency to judge with carrying around a suitcase of rocks on your head. He suggests that it feels wonderful when we stop judging, when we finally put the rocks down, and instead let each moment be just as it is. He describes this kind of letting go—or perhaps more accurately, letting be—as true liberation.

Sometimes it is tempting to try to feel good by condemn-

ing someone who is down and out because of their own failures. We may feel a strong pull to celebrate how superior we
are by hazing them when they have stumbled and can't defend
themselves particularly well, but there is something poisonous
about this. That poison is released in ourselves as well as on the
other person. Guilt and negativity, stemming from a deep realization that we have no business condemning others when we
have such great shortcomings ourselves, are not healthy properties to unleash. Our mind can become so preoccupied with
judging that there is little room for anything else.

Eventually this judgmental attitude will likely even target ourselves. We become so good at looking for the flaws, the
unworthiness in everyone and everything, that we are likely
to see all too clearly our own failings and to set in motion a
process of self-condemnation. When the habit of judging and
condemning is well developed, we have indeed established a
"mindless" self-defeating mental world in which to live and in
which the harm we do to ourselves is at least as great as that we
heap upon others.

Remember that Jesus also pointed out the benefits of forgiving instead of judging or condemning. Perhaps there is no
better way to win loyal support than to forgive someone, and
ironically this is especially true when they deserve our forgiveness the least. Of course Jesus is not arguing that we should
forgive in order to get something in return, but we will receive
a great deal if we do it sincerely. He is describing a natural process. We are human, too, and consequently we need a wide
margin of tolerance and forgiveness ourselves. Forgive others
and you will receive forgiveness. Give to others and you will be
given to in large amounts (in fact, in huge, running-over measure), Jesus says.

Interestingly, a popular prescription, offered over the years by a number of self-help authors and speakers (Zig Ziglar, for example) is that we should try to help people get what they need if we want to get what we need. This message is very consistent with a key part of the passage from Luke 6: *"for the measure you give will be the measure you get back."* That is, the very act of serving others can set in motion the dynamics that can assure that we will get all that we want. If we offer the best service to clients that enables them to get what they need, our services will be in great demand and we will prosper. If we consistently help others solve their troubling problems, we can feel confident that our position will be safe, that we will have security in what we do. If we are generous with others, including sharing our forgiveness when they need it, we will be treated generously and be forgiven ourselves.

While we may find exceptions to these statements in specific cases, for the most part they describe true relationships over time because others will tend to treat us better and we will treat ourselves better when we make a habit of forgiving rather than condemning. In other words, don't be quick to judge others. That will only create hate and judgment toward you. Instead, sincerely help others to improve and succeed. As a result not only will you be able to survive failure without condemnation, but you will also enjoy high regard, support, and prosperity. This is the simple lesson Jesus seems to be teaching.

FORGIVENESS, NOT CONDEMNATION,

WILL AFFIRM FOLLOWERS AND

CREATE A FRIENDLY SURFACE FOR LEADERS

TO FALL ON WHEN THEY STUMBLE

GATHER THE LOST SHEEP

What do you think? If a shepherd has a hundred sheep, and one of them has gone astray, does he not leave the ninety-nine on the mountains and go in search of the one that went astray? And if he finds it, truly I tell you, he rejoices over it more than over the ninety-nine that never went astray. (Matt. 18: 12–13)

A hard lesson is presented here. In recent recessionary times of downsizing, rightsizing, reengineering, or whatever other labels have been used to refer to massive employee layoffs, Jesus' challenge that not one person be willingly forfeited is a striking contrast. In fact, Jesus argues that the one person who is found, helped, and supported is of greater importance than all the others who were kept safely in the fold all along. This is hard mental medicine. It flies in the face of the rationale that says that losing a few people in order to keep the ship afloat (to keep the organization solvent) is a justified act. Jesus proclaims that every last person is priceless and deserving of great celebration.

This raises a great challenge for leadership. Shouldn't a leader be able to maintain an objective, cold, rational view, at least some of the time, in order to realize good business sense? (Or should she attempt to retain all employees even if it means making huge sacrifices?) Shouldn't a leader be able to make hard rational decisions in order to compete in a global economy and society? (Or should compassion and caring be his primary guides?) Aren't people sometimes expendable in the rages of economic war, as are so many soldiers in battles that are waged to serve a just cause? (Or is every person so valuable that everything possible should be done to save everyone?) Aren't individual players of little or no significance in the wider scheme of things? Aren't people really expendable in order to implement the master strategy, to reach the ultimate goal? Jesus demurs.

In fact, Jesus even emphasized the same point with a further illustration:

> *Or what woman having ten silver coins, if she loses one of them, does not light a lamp, sweep the house and search carefully until she finds it? When she has found it, she calls together her friends and neighbors, saying, "Rejoice with me, for I have found the coin that I had lost."*
> (Luke 15: 8–9)

Even though in these stories Jesus talks about sheep and coins, he was primarily concerned with the welfare of people and saving human souls. He frequently used metaphors to talk about people. Over and over he directed people to love their neighbor (their fellow humans) as themselves. That's why the relevance of this lesson seems so clear. He proclaims that not one person is to be cast aside as though they have no value. Each should be treated as though they were precious (every bit as precious as we ourselves are).

Thus, he points to a powerful leadership attitude—an attitude that views every single follower as worthy and valuable, as worth celebrating with great joy when they are held safely in or brought back into the fold. Leaders should look on the welfare of each follower as they would look on their own. To true leaders, every person they lead is priceless. No other organizational resource is of greater value.

One of my most dramatic experiences as a consultant occurred as a result of a management training program on employee self-leadership I conducted for a large American corporation. One manager really took the ideas I presented on self-leadership to heart. One of his subordinates was a production supervisor who was having such severe performance problems that he was about to be fired. The supervisor was having a variety of behavior problems and was also battling alcoholism. He clearly was lost, and the organization apparently had decided he was probably not worth saving.

Following my presentation, the manager decided to demonstrate confidence and faith in the supervisor by delegating as much responsibility as possible to him. He even made up excuses to leave the plant so he could put the supervisor in charge. I must confess that as the manager relayed this story to the training group in one of our sessions I was quite uncomfortable. I was trying to help the managers develop skills for gradually developing self-leadership and independence in followers—not for throwing followers into self-leadership situations with little or no skill development and guidance.

Nevertheless, the supervisor displayed a dramatic and almost immediate turnaround. He began behaving responsibly; he displayed initiative and pride in his work. The manager reported that the supervisor had gone from being about the worst supervisor in the plant to being arguably the best within about a two-week period. Several other managers in the session supported this assessment. They all looked dumbfounded at the change that had occurred. The manager said that the supervisor had even stopped drinking, the first progress they had seen him make on his alcohol problem in years.

An anecdote like this should of course be kept in perspective. It is just one case, and perhaps an anomaly at that. In addition, I have not been in touch with the plant for some time, so I am not sure the change was permanent. Nevertheless, I have observed too many similar incidents in my consulting to dismiss it as a fluke. I have been amazed at how many difficult and seemingly hopeless people can lead themselves out of their destructive ruts when given a chance and a little support. Very often those people we feel least compelled to embrace and support are precious diamonds in the rough that simply need to be polished with a little loving support and concern. As Jesus would point out, they are precious and well worth bringing back into the fold.

At this point, there is a temptation for some of us to react with outrage or perhaps disgust: "How naive or unrealistic can you get? An organization wouldn't last for a month with such a bleeding-heart perspective. No one had better apply for a leadership position in my firm with that kind of attitude." Or maybe we might respond with a bit softer stance: "That's all good from a moral and humanistic standpoint, but the realities of a competitive business environment make the philosophy infeasible. In the end, economic facts, not humanistic ideals, must take precedence in order for the most people to benefit."

Whatever your immediate reaction, the successes of numerous organizations with philosophies ever closer to what Jesus suggests are compelling. Many organizations have been empowering workers, often in team-based environments, and acknowledging their unique value and contributions.[1] The list of companies that have significantly embraced this kind of approach somewhere in their organization over the last few decades reads like a corporate who's who: General Motors, Ford, Motorola, General Electric, American Express, Herman Miller, W. L. Gore , Honeywell, Procter & Gamble, Cummins Engine, Digital Equipment, Boeing, Caterpillar, Texas Instruments, Gaines, AT&T, Xerox, LTV Steel, Tektronix—the list goes on and on, extending well beyond traditional large corporations to include numerous small businesses, health care organizations, universities, and even government agencies. Frequently they have empowered employees to make crucial decisions that affect not only the quality of their own work life but also the overall performance of the organization.

Vision and mission statements of very large and competitive corporations have often reflected this approach. Over the years I have had participants in my MBA classes and training programs share excerpts from their own company's statement, and in many cases (often in the companies that have better weathered economic downturns) significant emphasis has been placed on the organization's people as a particularly valuable resource. For example, a key part of Ford Motor Company's turnaround strategy from the brink of bankruptcy in the 1980s centered on the introduction of their statement, "Mission, Values and Guiding Principles," which describes people as "the source of our strength. They provide our corporate intelligence and determine our reputation and vitality. Involvement and teamwork are our core human values." It goes on to say that "employee involvement is our way of life—we are a team. We must treat each other with trust and respect." Given this fundamental perspective, it is perhaps no surprise that, when recent economic difficulties hit, Ford was the only American auto company to avoid bankruptcy.

Our cynical side may speak up at this point: "But vision statements are usually just a bunch of empty verbiage; they are not living documents in the organization." Conversely, some companies have gone so far as to make such a philosophy the ultimate goal and criterion for success. One classic example of this orientation is provided by the experience of AES Corporation, an independent energy producer during its emergence as a significant organization in the energy industry in the 1980s and 90s.[2] AES, at the time on the *Fortune* list of America's 100 fastest-growing companies, was primarily guided by four overriding values: (1) to act with integrity, (2) to be fair, (3) to have fun, and (4) to be socially responsible. The focus on fairness, for example, means treating fairly all people who are affected by the company—employees, customers, suppliers, stockholders, governments, and members of the community in which it operates. It attempts to leave out no one; everyone is treated as though he or she is of great value. In fact, Dennis Bakke, then the company's president, said that he did not pursue getting the most out of the company's negotiations to the detriment of the others involved. Instead, during exchanges with employees, supervisors, customers, and so on, he asked himself if he would feel as good in the other person's shoes as he did in his own.

AES's emphasis on its other primary values revealed a similar focus on human worth. In terms of fun, for example, Bakke explained that the company aimed to create an environment in which people could use their skills to serve important societal needs and consequently enjoy working at AES. The focus on social responsibility led to a goal of being good citizens of the world by operating safely, with increasing (not decreasing) employment opportunities, and helping to create a cleaner environment. Bakke explained that the company tried to behave as it would want its neighbor to behave. Finally, the emphasis on integrity pulled it all together by encouraging employees to pursue truthfulness and consistency in all they do.

There have been times during my many years of studying and consulting for organizations that Jesus' words have initially struck me as impractical, as something fine for Sunday mornings at church but not suitable for surviving in a world full of imperfect human beings. Fortunately, the many real-life stories of companies like Ford and AES have pushed me to rethink my periodic attacks of cynicism.

Jesus may not have had business success specifically in mind when he presented his challenging lesson on treating every person as uniquely valuable and worthy of celebration. Nevertheless, his timeless wise lessons appear to be robust, even in the face of the realities of cold business competition and economic difficulties. Leaders must lead with sound judgment and good common sense. Perhaps the most sensible philosophy they can hold to guide their decisions is to consider every human being as a priceless work of art that they must treat as worthy and valuable. In so doing, the greatest human (and frequently even economic) good will likely be achieved.

A TRUE MEASURE OF COMPASSIONATE

LEADERSHIP IS THE CARE LEADERS GIVE

TO THE LEAST OF THEIR FOLLOWERS

PART THREE

LEAD OTHERS TO
BE THEIR BEST SELVES

Real leadership comes from within.
Each of us can be our own ultimate
best leader. Wise leaders lead others
to lead themselves.

PREPARE THE SOIL

A sower went out to sow. And as he sowed, some seeds fell on the path, and the birds came and ate them up. Other seeds fell on rocky ground, where they did not have much soil, and they sprang up quickly, since they had no depth of soil. But when the sun rose, they were scorched; and since they had no root, they withered away. Other seeds fell among thorns, and the thorns grew up and choked them. Other seeds fell on good soil and brought forth grain, some a hundredfold, some sixty, some thirty. (Matt. 13: 3–8)

In this parable, Jesus provides a metaphor that can shed light on one of the most important aspects of leadership: laying the groundwork for positive influence and change. His teaching suggests how important it is to prepare the soil for the seeds of leadership. Indeed, many potential followers will simply not be ready for positive influence, even when serving with the best of leaders. This chapter reflects on the formidable challenge of preparing others for positive influence and change.

Change is one of the most feared and avoided phenomena in life. Most people simply are not comfortable with change and will resist it in a variety of ways. Consequently, attempting to lead others to positive change is an undertaking that deserves some serious consideration. One of the best models for understanding the challenging process of change was developed by Kurt Lewin. His work on the change process provides some useful guidance to leaders. Specifically, he outlined a very clear and logical three-step process.[1]

The most important step for this lesson is the first—*unfreezing*—which involves thawing out the rigid status quo. The focus is on preparing for the possibility of change. Jesus' teaching emphasizes the significance of the nature of the soil that receives the seeds. Some ideas simply cannot be accepted by some people at a given point in their lives. Surely a rock cannot receive a seed. But Lewin's model suggests that we can think in terms of ice rather than rocks. If current rigid attitudes and resistance can be set free—unfrozen—then positive influence and change is made possible. This might involve, for example, providing information that shows a gap between current and more desirable behaviors and practices, and allowing those people who are most affected to participate in planning the change. As a consultant, I have encountered this in many organizations. Once management is able to communicate the need for and opportunities of a change clearly and credibly, a formerly resistant workforce often opens up to considering and then supporting new approaches.

Once the unfreezing stage is completed, the second step can be taken—*moving or changing* behaviors, values, and/or attitudes. A leader might introduce the desired change with the aid of new organizational structures, procedures, or training, for example.

Finally, the third step—*refreezing*—involves introducing factors that lock in the new approach. For example, the leader could rely on incentives, systems, policies, structures, or norms to promote the continuation of the desired change.

The importance of unfreezing cannot be overemphasized.

As Jesus clearly points out, soil that is not ready to receive the seeds in a healthy way will render the sowing useless. Sometimes this reality has been well understood by organizations and their leaders and careful steps have been taken to assure that the soil is prepared for change. One of the best examples of this that I have encountered occurred in the mutual fund operations of an organization that later became a part of American Express.[2] A decision was made to change to an empowered work-team approach for servicing the division's clients (primarily independent financial planners). To prepare for the change, eleven people, representing a cross section of the division, were selected from volunteers to work full-time on designing and planning for the team system. This design team addressed issues and concerns of the employees and identified ways to be responsive to these needs in a team environment.

The process took more than eight months, and then a pilot team was launched to try out the design and work out the bugs in the system. When teams were finally rolled out across the entire organization months later, performance was excellent: quality indicators immediately shot up, backlogs seemed to disappear, and productivity increased significantly. Many problems were encountered along the way, but the organization's soil had been well prepared. Consequently, the teams seemed genuinely determined to make sure that the system worked well from the very beginning. One of the managers enthusiastically summed it up: "This team concept really works!"

When I was a young boy in Michigan, my friends and I enjoyed building snowmen. We learned that they would last longer if we poured water over them, which froze to a hard coating of ice. This created difficulty later. If we wanted to alter our work (let's say, to make a snow dog), we had to unfreeze the outer surface. Helping people change is difficult, whether they are made of snow or flesh, because they are (we all are), at least to some degree, struggling, fearful, resistant human beings who have formed hardened outer shells for self-defense. But with careful attention to preparing the soil (to unfreezing), the seeds of leadership can bear good fruit.

Jesus did go on to explain what he meant in his story about the seeds. His explanation provides further insight into the importance of preparing followers for leadership influence to make a positive change. He said,

> Hear then the parable of the sower. When anyone hears the word of the kingdom and does not understand it, the evil one comes and snatches away what is sown in the heart; this is what was sown on the path. As for what was sown on rocky ground, this is the one who hears the word and immediately receives it with joy; yet such a person has no root, but endures only for a while, and when trouble or persecution arises on account of the word, that person immediately falls away. As for what was sown among thorns, this is the one who hears the word, but the cares of the world and the lure of wealth choke the word, and it yields nothing. But as for what was sown on good soil, this is the one who hears the word and understands it, who indeed bears fruit and yields, in one case a hundredfold, in another sixty, and in another thirty. (Matt. 13: 18–23)

In this passage Jesus describes three important reasons why people may be unable to respond to constructive influence in working toward positive changes. *Ignorance* is one important barrier. Oftentimes people just don't see the logic of why something needs to be done or changed. Another barrier is an *unrealistic understanding* of the effort and sacrifice that are involved. As the old saying goes, most things that are worth doing don't come easily, or, more simply, no pain, no gain. If people are going to respond faithfully and serve with a leader, they need not only to embrace the cause but also to understand the difficulty that will be faced and be prepared to hang in there when the going gets tough. Finally, Jesus also points to the distractions of *other cares and concerns.* Is the undertaking that the leader is pointing to enough of a priority that it doesn't get lost in the barrage of other endless pressures and priorities? In summary, Jesus' story suggests that leaders need to promote clarity, realistic expectations, and the priority of the undertaking.

Maybe the most important lesson overall is that leaders should not expect much of a result from their leadership if they don't lay the necessary groundwork first. That is, we should not expect a very good crop if we haven't prepared the soil. Once again, this view shifts the focus away from the leader and toward others. If a person is sincere about wanting to be a positive force for change—an effective leader—the focus needs to be on the others who are involved. The leaders in the mutual fund operation mentioned above seemed to understand this leadership wisdom. Striking dramatic poses in front of the masses or in front of the mirror will not accomplish much, nor will inspiring rhetoric and captivating visions that don't address the specific needs and concerns of the persons being led. Rather, sincerely trying to help, support, and enable others to embrace and pursue worthwhile changes from a solid base of understanding, realistic expectations, and priority is the key. From this solid base the necessary unfreezing that enables change and refreezing may be possible.

THE SEEDS OF LEADERSHIP WILL GROW ONLY

IN SOIL THAT IS PREPARED TO ACCEPT THEM

BE FORGIVING—ALLOW MISTAKES FOR THE SAKE OF LEARNING

There was a man who had two sons. The younger of them said to his father, "Father, give me the share of the property that will belong to me." So he divided his property between them. A few days later the younger son gathered all he had and traveled to a distant country, and there he squandered his property in dissolute living. When he had spent everything, a severe famine took place throughout that country, and he began to be in need. So he went and hired himself out to one of the citizens of that country, who sent him to his fields to feed the pigs. He would gladly have filled himself with the pods that the pigs were eating; and no one gave him anything. But when he came to himself he said, "How many of my father's hired hands have bread enough and to spare, but here I am dying of hunger! I will get up and go to my father, and I will say to him, 'Father, I have sinned against heaven and before you; I am no longer worthy to be called your son; treat me like one of your hired hands.'" So he set off and went to his father. But while he was still far off, his father saw him and was filled with compassion; he ran and put his arms around him and kissed him. Then the son said to him, "Father, I have sinned against heaven and before you; I am no longer

*worthy to be called your son." But the father said to his slaves,
"Quickly, bring out a robe—the best one—and put it on him;
put a ring on his finger and sandals on his feet. And get the
fatted calf and kill it, and let us eat and celebrate; for this
son of mine was dead and is alive again; he was lost and is
found!" And they began to celebrate.* (Luke 15: 11–24)

Jesus' captivating story of the return of the prodigal son is perhaps his most poignant lesson on forgiveness and compassion.
In a very real sense the son's request for his share of his father's
inheritance while the father was still alive was a wish that his
father were dead. He did not want to wait for his father to live
out his life with the benefit of what he had earned. He wanted
his share now. On top of this the son took his inheritance and
spent it all on a reckless pleasure binge. He left his family be-
hind and threw himself into a life focused on self-gratification.
He had essentially left his father as though his father were dead.
Indeed, strong justification existed for the father simply to dis-
own the son. The son's offense was extremely great. When the
son finally came to his senses, even he no longer saw himself
fit to be called a son.

When the son returned, however, he found his father waiting not with condemnation but with open arms. The father
clothed and comforted the son. He declared that the son had
been dead but was alive again. He was joyous and ready to
celebrate. What does this amazing story teach us about life and
leadership?

First, Jesus seems to be indicating that if we really care for others, then perhaps no offense is too great to be worthy of forgiveness and compassion if the offender has truly repented and is ready to change—that is, if the person has honestly faced his mistakes and is ready to redirect himself. In some cases it may take suffering the consequences of a dramatic mistake to truly prepare someone to bear real fruit. Such an experience can provide the foundation for a renewed commitment to constructive self-leadership. In a sense, a hard slap in the face can be applied by the challenge of life and one's failure in handling it. But this so-called failure can provide a powerful motivation to change. It is far too easy to continue in the same rut and to apply the same personal strategies indefinitely unless something dramatic occurs. That is why, ironically, when people suffer dramatic failures that are clearly of their own doing and recognize and acknowledge their responsibility, it may be the best time to provide encouragement and support rather than condemnation. At last the boil has been lanced, and they are ready to be healed. The father in Jesus' story seems to realize all this. To him, his son had been the one who was dead, but now he is ready to start living again.

Second, the story seems to emphasize the value of learning, even in the face of an egregious and horrific failure. The son finally learned the value of being a son, which he had previously so lightly thrown aside. Now he was ready to seek forgiveness sincerely and to serve even as a slave. The son's imperfect humanity was blatantly exposed for all to see. Yet through the experience he had gained valuable insight. He had perhaps gained the knowledge he needed to establish the foundation for a worthwhile life.

One of my favorite stories from organization folklore reportedly occurred at IBM.[1] A senior executive made a very poor decision that cost the company millions of dollars. When called to the CEO's office, he logically expected to be harshly dismissed from his position. He entered the office cautiously and engaged in a conversation with the CEO. Eventually, beginning to become bewildered, he raised the topic that he most feared but assumed was inevitable: he asked if he was to be fired. The CEO's response was very insightful and apparently wise. The essence of what he said was, simply, "Fire you? No way. We just spent several million dollars educating you." This leader seemed to understand the lesson Jesus was teaching.

Jesus' lesson, however, does not end here. Now let's take a look at the rest of the story:

> *Now his elder son was in the field; and when he came and approached the house, he heard music and dancing. He called one of the slaves and asked what was going on. He replied, "Your brother has come, and your father has killed the fatted calf, because he has got him back safe and sound." Then he became angry and refused to go in. His father came out and began to plead with him. But he answered his father, "Listen! For all these years I have been working like a slave for you, and I have never disobeyed your command; yet you have never given me even a young goat so that I might celebrate with my friends. But when this son of yours came back, who has devoured your property with prostitutes, you killed the fatted calf for him!" Then the father said to him, "Son, you are always with me, and all that is mine is yours. But we had to celebrate and rejoice, because this brother of yours was dead and has come to life; he was lost and has been found."* (Luke 15: 25–31)

Thus, as if the story about the younger son was not enough, Jesus introduces yet another plot surrounding the older and apparently more righteous son. This son had remained loyal, serving the father for many years. He seemingly had a legitimate reason to be angry. The younger son, who had not remained loyal or sacrificed alongside him, was apparently being rewarded for irresponsible behavior. But the father expresses love for the older son and tries to teach him about what is most important—putting the welfare of his brother (others) first, particularly when his brother is in most need of help.

This part of the story teaches us the importance of pursuing virtuous ideals such as service, compassion, and forgiveness for their own value. This is consistent with the teachings of the Greek philosopher Aristotle, who taught that the greatest good comes from that which is an end in itself. The father in the story has nothing to gain by forgiving and caring for his son, except the experience of being compassionate and receiving back the son who had essentially tossed him aside. Jesus seems to be teaching us that, ironically, those things in life that we doggedly pursue to serve ourselves (wealth, power, fame) never seem to be fully obtained and enjoyed. It is often when we lose ourselves for a worthwhile cause, particularly for the benefit of others, that at last the inner rewards of acting nobly are enjoyed.

This has been a persistent theme in the applications of empowerment around the world. The real power of empowering others in the workplace seems to flow from the psychological sense of ownership that employees experience when they are sincerely included in the decision making and leading of the organization. When organization members become preoccupied with concrete personal payoffs, the potential financial and other material rewards of playing the system, empowerment is rendered largely impotent. The burning fire of a passionate commitment to the work system to which employees belong—and which in a very real sense belongs to the employees—is the primary fuel that enables the system to become empowering. The father in the story felt this passion and expressed it through compassion. And the younger son was beginning to feel it as well.

Thus, a transactor mentality, in which we calculatedly do what we believe is right in order to obtain a concrete return for ourselves, is never quite satisfying. The older brother was bitter because his loyalty and faithfulness to his father had apparently gone unrewarded. He wanted a concrete payoff for his work and service. Yet the father responded by pointing out that all that he had already belonged to the older son. Perhaps if the older son had really understood this he would have naturally celebrated his brother's return.

Henri Nouwen wrote an entire book on Rembrandt's masterpiece painting portraying the return of the prodigal son and on how it changed and provided direction for his own life.[2] He suggested that each of us likely experiences the roles of both the pleasure-seeking younger son and the self-righteous older son at some time in our life. The real challenge he points to is that of growing into the compassionate father who supports and affirms others.

As Nouwen did, I traveled to St. Petersburg, Russia, and was able to see the original large and impressive painting at the Hermitage museum. I also journeyed to Amsterdam and visited Rembrandt's former home, where he had lived during the more prosperous years of his career. I learned that eventually Rembrandt had lost this beautiful house because he had not been able to keep up with the payments. Nouwen suggests that Rembrandt may well have progressed through the role of the younger and older son and finally to the father in later years, after experiencing a life focused on pleasure followed by personal and financial tragedy. By the time he painted his masterpiece, the Return of the Prodigal Son, presumably Rembrandt had finally become much like the father in the story.

Nouwen challenges each of us to identify which of the characters in the story we are most like. I found the painting itself filled with emotion and meaning. In ways that I think are similar to what Nouwen experienced, it brought the story to life for me and provided a kind of window to the soul.

Perhaps the overall lesson we can learn from Jesus' story is that the best kind of leadership is often an act of self-sacrificing compassion. Because leaders have no one else to lead but flawed, imperfect, even hurtful human beings, forgiveness and compassion are essential tools in the leadership toolbox. And yet they cannot be tools intended to twist or turn some leader-desired payoff. If they are to produce optimal results, they are best offered as gifts that unleash the potential good and worth of others. At times leaders must empower others by forgiving them and allowing them to have a second, third, and even fourth chance.

A MARK OF A LEADER IS THE

ABILITY TO FORGIVE AND THEN SEE THE

OPPORTUNITIES FOR LEARNING IN

THE MISTAKES OF FOLLOWERS

LEAD BY SERVING

*You know that among the Gentiles those whom they
recognize as their rulers lord it over them, and their great ones
are tyrants over them. But it is not so among you; but
whoever wishes to become great among you must be your
servant, and whoever wishes to be first among you must
become the slave of all.* (Mark 10: 42–44)

This is clearly one of the more striking passages from Jesus'
teachings related to leadership. In fact, it turns leadership up-
side down. The lesson seems to be that to become a great leader you should act as a servant, not as a commander or even
as a charismatic source of inspiration. The idea is indeed puz-
zling and challenging, but Jesus repeats the same basic message
several times in his teachings. He instructs that if you want to
become great, be humble, sit in the lowest places of honor,
become like a child. Again, Jesus challenges us to rethink what
it means to be a leader. He challenges us to resist the temptation to act out a leadership role of being superior to others and
behaving as though we know it all.

Judith Neal, formerly Executive Director of the Association
for Spirit at Work and currently Director of the Tyson Center for
Faith and Spirituality at the University of Arkansas, described a
striking practice that can help foster the managerial mindset of
being a servant. It originated from the Tomasso Corporation,
a highly successful food processing plant located in Montreal,

Canada.[1] The practice has been called "A Gesture." It was inspired by J. Robert Ouimet, Chairman of the Board of the holding company that owns Tomasso, who is very dedicated to the idea that economic well-being and human well-being go hand in hand. "A Gesture" involved the management team going together to serve food to the poor 2 to 3 times a year. After serving the meal, they would sit down with the people they had served to talk with them and to get to know them more personally. Later, when they returned to the plant, the managers met to talk about what the experience meant to them. Over time, other employees in the plant asked if they could participate as well. Eventually anyone who wanted to could attend "A Gesture" which took place during regular work hours and was considered paid time.

The idea of servant leadership has been written about at length by Robert Greenleaf, author and founder of the Greenleaf Center for Servant-Leadership.[2] He postulated that true leaders are those who lead by serving others. He argued that potential followers will "respond only to individuals who are chosen as leaders because they are proven and trusted as servants."[3] He also stated that as followers are served by servant leaders they "become healthier, wiser, freer, more autonomous, more likely themselves to become servant leaders."[4]

Being a servant is fairly straightforward: look for others' needs and try to help meet them. The Golden Rule—*do to others as you would have them do to you*—is a strong anchoring principle here, as it is with so many of the leadership lessons Jesus has offered. Of course, we need to feel confident that we serve in a way that is beneficial to others for the long term. We don't want to create weakness and overdependence in others by catering to them in the short run in a way that is potentially harmful to their long-term growth and development.

Herman Miller, Inc. (mentioned in a previous chapter), a leading innovator and manufacturer in the business furniture industry, places special importance on all employees and the role they can play for serving the organization and one another.[5] Near the entrance to the company's Design Yard (housing the design studio and executive offices) is a statue called "Watercarrier." It reflects the Native American belief in the significant role of every task performed by every person for serving the community. In 1987, former CEO Max De Pree began the tradition of identifying some members of Herman Miller as Watercarriers, emphasizing their service to new employees in passing on the essence of the institution. Max De Pree's father, D. J. De Pree, was selected as the first Watercarrier and hundreds of others (whose names are all displayed in a reflecting pool) have been selected since. At Herman Miller, the image of an individual carrying water for his community creates a clear image that symbolizes direct service of others.

One of the most challenging contemporary leadership roles calls for an approach that is consistent with the idea of providing beneficial service to others. I'm talking about the role of *empowered team leaders.* Teams can be found everywhere today, and they are viewed by many organizations as the key to tapping the full mental and physical capabilities of the workforce. The fundamental philosophy is that if employees are provided with all the resources and information they need, they will solve work problems in creative and productive ways that will be superior to the results of a traditional bureaucracy, and they will consequently find their work more rewarding and grow as individuals. In other words, let workers on teams stand on their own two feet if you want them to be all they can be.

Recently a special issue in the journal *Organizational*

Dynamics was published on the topic of "The Ins and Outs of Leading Teams."[6] The articles that appeared were written by some of the world's leading authorities on the topic and focused on a range of issues including leading virtual teams, leading teams in the boardroom, and leading team connections and boundaries. In the capstone article written by the editors, the common theme identified across the various articles appearing in the special issue was the idea of shared leadership—a dynamic, interactive influence process where the people involved lead one another (including both designated leaders and followers) toward common goals.[7] This perspective essentially redefines the nature of leadership as a social process (rather than a role performed by an individual who happens to be identified as a "leader") that hinges on persons stepping forward to lead when their expertise and experience is needed and stepping back and allowing others to lead when the current task requires their expertise. This means that the person who is considered the formal leader will at times be stepping out of the way to allow so called "followers" to lead when their input is most needed…and some of the time, in effect, the formal leader becomes a follower.

All of these new ways of thinking about and approaching the practice of leadership can create some confusing and difficult challenges for team leaders. For example, when Lake Superior Paper Company in Duluth, Minnesota, launched empowered teams they had a plan to have supervisors gradually fade into the background. They planned for this role to evolve from direct supervision of the teams to a position of shared authority and eventually to a facilitator external to the team. The lack of traditional authority made these would-be facilitator leaders feel squeezed between upper management and the teams. One individual described this team leader role as a kind of buffer that "gets it from both ways."[8] There was also a fear among a number of team leaders that they risked working themselves out of a job if they served the teams successfully enough so that the team was able to become effectively empowered.

Similarly, in the mutual fund operations of the organization that became part of American Express, mentioned in the chapter called "Prepare the Soil," a team leader lamented, "There's nothing to call my own. Eventually, if they're truly self-managing, it's going to be the team that gets most of the recognition. Traditionally the recognition that the unit's doing good would start with the supervisor." Another leader added, "I really would enjoy it if just occasionally somebody would pat me on the back and say, 'Hey, you're doing a good job today.'"[9]

The team leader role is no longer to direct and manage, nor is it to step in and solve everything for the team. Instead, leaders become developers and helpers. They become individuals who enable teams to do their best by making sure they have what they need and by providing them with the leeway to do what they decide to do. Essentially, good team leaders become servants. Instead of wielding power, they empower. But they must be careful not to breed too much dependence on themselves by the teams. They must learn to avoid giving the answers and solving the problems. If the teams are going to succeed, they must learn to do these things for themselves.

Many traditional supervisors are not able to make the transition successfully when their organization decides to implement teams. The ones who do succeed have to rethink what it is to be a good leader. No longer are they the king or queen of the hill, nor do they dominate the spotlight. Their job is to serve the people on the teams so they can accomplish their work and become better team members in the process. Team leaders must learn to feast on humble pie and to find their satisfaction in the team's success and recognition rather than in their own. I have observed many effective team leaders encouraging and supporting their teams and ensuring that they have all the resources, information, and training they need to do their work well. Ultimately the truly successful leaders become good servants who help their team members meet their own needs.

Despite the challenges in carrying out this servant role, many team leaders have found it to be quite rewarding. One Lake Superior Paper leader was particularly gratified by the enthusiastic response of team members to his serving approach within the team system: "I could never go back [to a traditional autocratic system]. I saw all the wasted potential. . . . Here if you ask if someone will do something, you get three people stuck in the door volunteering for it. They're really gung ho."[10] Another team leader explained that he just enjoys the act of serving rather than controlling. "Now I get more satisfaction out of helping someone to do something rather than telling them to do it."[11]

Being a humble servant is the path to greatness that Jesus points to. He served as a highly visible model of servant leadership himself. Perhaps his most concrete example of servant leadership occurred during his last supper with his disciples (his own team).

And during supper Jesus . . . got up from the table, took off his outer robe, and tied a towel around himself. Then he poured water into a basin and began to wash the disciples' feet and to wipe them with the towel that was tied around him.

After he had washed their feet, had put on his robe and

*had returned to the table, he said to them, "Do you know what
I have done to you? You call me Teacher and Lord—and you
are right, for that is what I am. So if I, your Lord and Teacher,
have washed your feet, you ought to wash one another's feet.
For I have set you an example, that you also should do as I have
done to you.* (John 13: 2–5, 12–15)

Clearly Jesus had no intention of being the only servant
leader. He demonstrated and then urged his disciples to do the
same. There is a major difference between trying to dominate
the leadership spotlight for your own glorification and encouraging others to take an active role in the leadership process.
Jesus seems to be leading others—or in this case perhaps we
should say serving others—to lead themselves to service. This
is a powerful leadership idea because it provides the necessary
ingredients for a vast spreading of the process throughout the
population. It offers the potential to enlist a whole army of servants who are able to consider the well-being of others rather
than just their own personal gain. Thus, servant-focused leadership not only transcends the leader's own temptation to fall
prey to leadership myths (such as that leaders should know all
the answers, receive all the fame and glory, and so on) but also
encourages others to do the same.

REAL LEADERS ARE HUMBLE SERVANTS,

NOT POWER-HUNGRY TYRANTS

LEAD WITHOUT BLINDNESS

They are blind guides of the blind. And if one blind person guides another, both will fall into a pit. (Matt. 15: 14)

Jesus presents a simple commonsense idea in this passage. It contains a lesson that is well worth considering deeply by anyone who aspires to lead others. It raises important questions such as the following: Are you about to lead others blindly into a pit? Are your followers better equipped to lead themselves than to follow you? Do people who live with their problems day in and day out see their situation more clearly than anyone else? How blind are you to the real issues that need to be addressed in this leadership situation? Can you lead others to see their own situations more clearly so they can practice more effective self-leadership? Is the ultimate act of leadership to facilitate others so they can lead themselves? Is it presumptuous, maybe even preposterous, to assume that an external leader can exercise leadership that is more effective than that person's own self-leadership?

A trust walk is a classic interpersonal development exercise. The usual procedure involves blindfolding a person, then grasping the blindfolded person's arm and leading him on a walk. At first this is usually an awkward situation for the person who cannot see. He tends to take very slow, awkward steps as he tries to feel for potential objects or changes in the terrain that might trip him up. Even though he is being guided by a person who can clearly see where they are walking, a lack of trust makes the going difficult initially. Eventually, however, the blindfolded person realizes that everything is going fine, and that it is OK to relax and follow the lead of the guide. This is a simple but powerful exercise that provides a valuable lesson about learning to rely on someone else.

Unfortunately, navigating the obstacles and ruts in the road of life can be a lot more complicated than walking around an uncluttered room or a well-mowed yard. Even when a trust walk is conducted through a difficult and varied terrain, the guide can usually help the other person to manage quite well as long as the guide is able to see clearly. Imagine, however, what would happen if, even though the guide was ready and willing to lead, the route they were walking on really could not be seen clearly. Even more to the point, imagine what would happen if the guide was blindfolded and the walking course was filled with large holes, with pits, that were ready to swallow up anyone who took an improper step. This image is even more striking if the person being guided has developed trust and confidence that the guide sees clearly and that no harm will come to them.

The issue of whether a designated leader is really a blind guide is a terribly important one. Leaders have been blindly leading others into pits throughout history. Part of the reason for this situation is that our knowledge about how to lead others effectively is not very clear. Even today, after decades of research and thousands of studies, there is still no commonly agreed-upon approach to effective leadership. Theories abound. In fact, one well-regarded handbook of leadership written a couple decades ago that reviewed much of the leadership research up to that time was already so huge that the reference list alone was nearly two hundred pages long.[1] And since that time the amount of leadership research and writing has vastly increased. The magnitude and confusion of the leadership literature is itself blinding, even when a person sincerely studies it in the hope of avoiding being a blind leader. No matter how confident and convincing a leader is, all too often followers are better off if they simply ignore the leader and follow their own lead.

This brings us back to the current emphasis on worker empowerment. Repeatedly organizations are discovering that they are more successful if they remove layers and layers of leaders (or, if you prefer, managers) and place more of the leadership responsibility in the hands of those who previously were being led. People tend to learn a great deal about their own work, problems, and unique personal characteristics because they struggle with them more than anyone else. Often the best leader for people is ultimately themselves. In significant ways they are really the only ones who have learned enough to remove their blindfolds. This is a large part of why the concept of self-leadership (the process of influencing ourselves) has received increasing attention and recognition as a core aspect of leadership in both work and life.[2]

Thus the most effective leaders are often those who lead others to lead themselves. By guiding and developing people to be competent self-leaders, a leader is able to spread strength throughout the entire system. These self-leaders are then better equipped to make the decisions, with their eyes open, regarding how to make adjustments and improvements as they traverse the terrain (cope with the challenges) of daily work and life. Leaders continue to be very important, but more in facilitating self-leadership and less in shouldering the entire leadership burden.

Jesus' warning is a telling one. Arguably more than at any other time in history, the world is full of pits into which we may fall. At the same time, the drive to compete, succeed, wield power, become wealthy, and any number of other self-gratifying acts drives many to seek the influence and authority of being a leader. Too many of these would-be leaders see far more clearly their own potential personal gains than the ubiquitous pits that await them and their followers. Perhaps the most difficult blindfold to remove is the one that causes so many to place blind trust in others when they are capable of making far better choices for themselves. Ironically, that same blindfold enables those truly blinded leaders to project an illusion of 20/20 vision.

In the end, the primary lesson seems to be that it is we who would lead who most need to see clearly our tendency toward blindness. If we want to lead others, we must first learn to lead ourselves with unusual clarity. What do you believe equips you to lead others? Do you really understand the situations and obstacles that your followers face? We must carefully uncover and address our own vast failings and personal imperfections. In the process of completing such a self-examination we may discover the importance of relying on any sightedness that is available. We may also realize that usually no one sees his or her path more clearly than the one who has created and traversed it. It seems that the only leaders who are truly clear-sighted are the ones who know, when it comes to the specifics of the challenges faced by others, that they are really quite blind. Consequently, these true leaders are better equipped to lead others to lead themselves.

THE MOST CLEAR-SIGHTED LEADERS RECOGNIZE

THEIR OWN BLINDNESS AND INSTILL AND

RELY ON THE SELF-LEADERSHIP OF FOLLOWERS

THE VALUE OF PENNIES

He sat down opposite the treasury, and watched the crowd putting money in the treasury. Many rich people put in large sums. A poor widow came and put in two small copper coins, which are worth a penny. Then he called his disciples and said to them, "Truly I tell you, this poor widow has put in more than all those who are contributing to the treasury. For all of them have contributed out of their abundance; but she out of her poverty has put in everything she had, all she had to live on." (Mark 12: 41–44)

The issue of evaluating and responding to the contributions of others is a major challenge for leaders. It is usually considered effective leadership to distinguish levels of performance of followers and to dole out rewards according to the amount that is contributed. This approach seems to be rational, logical, and even just. But once again Jesus throws us a curve. The value of contributions, he seems to be saying, must be considered in light of the capabilities of the contributor.

Initially this may send up some red flags. Is the implication that we should not concern ourselves with the levels of our employees' performance? If someone means well and is doing the best she can and her performance is unsatisfactory, should a leader simply pat her on the back and praise her for trying? While this practice may not be as illogical as it sounds,

I don't think it is the real leadership lesson that can be learned. Perhaps the lesson is best summarized by prescribing a focus on the heart of the person. That is, pay attention to the intent, the motives, and the progress of the person. This may indeed be very sound wisdom for a couple of reasons.

First, this is generally a good philosophy because it is not only humane and ethical but also surprisingly beneficial to both parties, ultimately. The world is and has been throughout history replete with persons who have trampled human relationships in the pursuit of wealth and power. Sometimes those closest and most dear to us—favorite colleagues and even our immediate family members—have been tossed aside and ignored because of the allure of worldly attractions. We have all heard the often-repeated lament of successful persons at the pinnacle of their career saying they would give it all up in a moment to be able to relive the years they could have better spent with their loved ones. Good friendships and healthy family relationships usually turn out in the end to be far more precious than the gold or fame that spurs on our obsessive pursuit. While this theme may seem a bit sweet and syrupy, it represents a reality that is hard to deny if we face it honestly.

In addition, this philosophy can represent the foundation for good, practical human development and performance-facilitating leadership. That is, if the person's heart is in the right place, then the necessary skills and capabilities can likely be developed. How many times have you seen persons with seemingly tremendous talent and ability whose lives have crumbled on useless paths to nowhere because they lacked healthy commitment to anything worthwhile? A wise leader will look for the people who display a willingness to throw themselves into worthwhile pursuits, who are ready and eager to learn and do their best.

During twenty-five years of consulting and university teaching I have learned that surprisingly often the individuals who look to be the biggest rejects can become the best performers when they are given a chance. I have encountered numerous employees and students who blossomed into stars when they were provided with the guidance and training they needed to go along with their optimism and motivation. In many other cases they did not end up turning in the highest levels of performance in any absolute sense, but they became solid, even star team players because of the positive impact they had on others.

One of the most dramatic examples in this vein is the true story of Rudy Ruettiger.[1] Perhaps you have seen the inspiring movie based on his dream and ultimate realization of becoming a student and football player at Notre Dame. When he graduated from high school, with mediocre grades and no money, his chances seemed remote at best. After working for years and saving his money, he applied to Notre Dame but was rejected for the first of several times. Refusing to give up, he enrolled in a nearby community college, worked as a groundskeeper at Notre Dame, and kept reapplying until he was finally admitted.

Lacking size and talent, Rudy made the football team as a walk-on because of his enthusiasm and determination. After serving on the practice squad for two years, he was finally allowed to suit up and stand on the sidelines in the final game of his college football career. With seconds left in the game, and with many fans and players who had been inspired by his dedication calling his name, the coach put him in for the final play. In the only play of his career, he sacked the opposing quarterback for a loss. The team responded by carrying him off the field, an honor that has never since been repeated. Indeed, Rudy seemed to have little more than a penny's worth of talent and ability to contribute. But in the end he left an inspiring legacy that has been permanently recorded in Notre Dame history. In many ways he has inspired a more heroic image for Notre Dame football than the countless strong and talented football greats who have played before and after him. His is the story of a person of average size and talent whom typical fans can identify with and admire.

More recently, 61-year-old Tom Thompson, seemingly against all odds, endured repeated initial eligibility rejections from the NCAA, and then physical injuries, knee surgery, and strenuous training regimes during his college football training at Division III Austin College. For months, he worked out alongside players not only young enough to be his children but his grandchildren. When he finally entered a game in the fall of 2009 against rival Trinity College to kick an extra point, he became the oldest football player in NCAA history. The story of his gritty journey was widely picked up by the media—by the likes of *The Sporting News*, *Fox*, *CBS*, and *ESPN*, among many others—becoming a source of inspiration for many, perhaps especially those that find themselves in the fourth quarter of their own lives.

Motivated, conscientious, sincere, committed contributors will in the end likely serve and deliver far more than highly talented, indifferent natural stars. So what if some people can show off raw talent on a whimsical basis? Are they in it for the long haul? Are they really giving what they are capable of giving? Are we sensitive to the seemingly low-value contributions of conscientious, committed persons that may really represent vast treasures if we could only see them? These are the kinds of questions that Jesus urges us to ask. Most skills and abilities can be improved with the proper training and experience. So why not measure what people are doing relative to their current capabilities and spend special effort on assessing where their heart is? The real stars shine on the inside. Sometimes they are a lump of coal waiting to be transformed into a diamond. The solid material of the treasure often shines within rather than without.

Jesus calls us to develop a deeper vision—a vision of beauty in the effort and the sacrifice made by each person. He warns us not to be deceived by the shiny brightness of pretentious show-offs who can blind us to what is really valuable in people. He reminds us to look for the value of pennies that can be the basis for both moral and practical riches for years to come.

TRUE LEADERS FOCUS ON THE HEARTS OF

FOLLOWERS AND RECOGNIZE THAT SMALL

CONTRIBUTIONS MADE WITH SINCERITY CAN

FORM THE FOUNDATION FOR LARGE SUCCESSES

INSTILL COMMITMENT, NOT GREED

For the kingdom of heaven is like a landowner who went out early in the morning to hire laborers for his vineyard. After agreeing with the laborers for the usual daily wage, he sent them into his vineyard. When he went out about nine o'clock he saw others standing idle in the marketplace; and he said to them, "You also go into the vineyard, and I will pay you whatever is right." So they went. When he went out again about noon and about three o'clock, he did the same. And about five o'clock he went out and found others standing around; and he said to them, "Why are you standing here idle all day?" They said to him, "Because no one has hired us." He said to them, "You also go into the vineyard." When evening came, the owner of the vineyard said to his manager, "Call the laborers and give them their pay, beginning with the last and then going to the first." When those hired about five o'clock came, each of them received the usual daily wage. Now when the first came, they thought they would receive more; but each of them also received the usual daily wage. And when they received it, they grumbled against the landowner, saying, "These last worked only one hour, and you have made them equal to us who have borne the burden of the day and the scorching heat." But he replied to one of them, "Friend, I am doing you no wrong; did you not agree with me for the usual daily wage? Take what belongs to you and go; I choose to give

to this last the same as I give to you. Am I not allowed to do
what I choose with what belongs to me? Or are you envious
because I am generous?" (Matt. 20: 1–15)

One of the most widely advocated and supported principles
of effective influence of human behavior in the latter half of
the twentieth century is that people should be rewarded based
on their performance. That is, those who accomplish more
should receive more reward than those who do less. Basic reinforcement theory, most widely associated with the work of
B. F. Skinner in the field of psychology[1] and later adapted to
many settings, including work organizations, posits that reinforcement (desired rewards that strengthen targeted behaviors)
should be given contingent on performance of desired behaviors. Reinforcement theory says that the laborers who worked
all day should have received more (a lot more) than those who
worked only half the day, let alone those who worked only one
hour. Jesus' lesson seems to fly in the face of one of the most
supported and prescribed principles for leaders. In considering
this story, one is left wondering if anything that has commonly
guided contemporary leadership practice can be relied on.

To make matters worse, the story also directly challenges
the widely supported management perspective generally referred to as equity theory.[2] According to equity theory, people
will naturally compare the ratio of their inputs (performance,
effort, and so on) relative to the rewards they receive with
the input-to-reward ratio of others. If they perceive inequity,
especially when they are on the short end of the stick, they will
experience significant tension. Consequently, they will take action to correct the inequity, such as not exerting much effort or

quitting altogether. At first glance, Jesus' story just doesn't seem to make much sense in terms of what are generally presented as sound management principles—that is, we should reward people in proportion to what they do, and we should make the rewards equitable (fair) according to people's relative contributions.

So what gives? What is Jesus trying to teach here? I must confess that I began my research and consulting careers as a strong advocate of reinforcement theory and a supporter of equity theory. In that former life, my reaction to the implied lesson of the story would not have been very sympathetic—in fact, rejection and scoffing would probably be better descriptions. Since that time, however, I have seriously reconsidered my position. It is not so much that I believe principles related to reinforcement and equity no longer apply, but that relying on them too heavily can make things worse rather than better.

First, the carrot-and-stick approach has some severe limitations. Trying to lead—or more aptly, to manage (and some would even say manipulate)—highly intelligent, advanced creatures by providing rewards when they comply with our wishes can create a suboptimal process. Essentially, when we do this we are training people to be transactors. We teach them to search for the self-serving benefit of performing narrowly defined tasks. We teach them to be highly selective in what they do, and to be responsive to only one limited form of motivation (the rewards we offer) for doing it. We essentially train them to do the minimum of what we ask and to do so with their sights continually set on the reward they will receive. I can't help but think of the comical miniature bears I once saw performing in a Russian circus in St. Petersburg. After every time they climbed a ladder or walked a tightrope, they immediately ran offstage, on their hind legs of course (to the laughter of the crowd), to receive their food reward. People possess such vast mental richness and creativity that reducing them to a similar kind of transactor is not very comical; indeed, it is sad.

Second, a far more effective as well as humane approach to leadership centers on stimulating commitment (a willingness and eagerness to go above and beyond the call of duty) and psychological ownership (a sense that our input and creativity are valued and that in an important way we psychologically own the organization because we share in making it a success in which we can take pride). All this requires that trust be placed in leaders—that is, leaders need to earn the trust of followers, not just with words but through authentic empowering action that demonstrates they have followers' best interests in mind and are sincere in enlisting their involvement. People do need to be rewarded for what they do. They have to pay their bills and have some financial resources to live. They should be paid well for their contributions, and they should share in the organization's profits. They also need to receive praise and recognition for a job well done. But these rewards should not be the focus. If they are, people will become compliant transactors, not fully engaged, committed, growing human beings.

Many organizations are discovering that this commitment/ ownership orientation to leading employees can be far more effective than a transactional approach. For example, the innovative and highly successful W. L. Gore & Associates, producer of a variety of products from outdoor camping equipment to medical materials to industrial supplies, deemphasizes pay in favor of other sources of motivation for its workforce. Gore operates according to what it calls "unmanagement" and "unstructure," in which people are allowed to initiate projects on their own and to interact with whoever seems most appropriate to further their work, without going through a traditional chain of command. In fact, the empowered and committed workforce is so highly regarded that people are called associates, not employees. Gore has built its success squarely on the contributions of all of its people, without placing an undue focus on external rewards, especially financial ones. Sally Gore, daughter of the company's founder, put it this way: "We do not feel we need to be the highest paid. We never try to steal people away from other companies with salary. We want them to come here because of the opportunities for growth and the unique work environment."[3]

Equal Exchange, a for-profit democratic worker cooperative (one of the largest in the country), provides another striking example of a business that instills a spirit of commitment rather than greed in its workforce.[4] Every member of the organization, as in a democracy, is provided with an equal vote in the firm's governance, open access to information, freedom of speech, and an equitable share of the firm's distribution of resources (such as income). The organization itself is owned by the employees in equal shares, and employees also receive an equal share of profits and losses. These "worker-owners" elect a nine-seat Board of Directors and fill six of the seats themselves. The Board hires and supervises the firm's managers who make up the Office of Executive Directors. Thus, employees (at the "bottom"), as owners, are also at the top of the organization chart. And the organization uses a 4 to 1 maximum top to bottom pay ratio...that is, no person (including the CEO) can have pay that is more than four times that of the lowest-paid employee (compare this to ratios that are frequently in the hundreds—that is, executives at the top are paid hundreds of times more than bottom level employees—for more traditional organizations).

Further, as discussed earlier, more and more leaders and organizations have learned that one of the most powerful ways of facilitating an effective and committed workforce and organization is through empowered work teams. On teams, individual contributions are often rewarded on the basis of pay-for-knowledge systems. That is, the more skills employees master and demonstrate competence in, the more they are paid. While this can be a highly effective approach to encouraging learning, it can have some unfortunate side effects. For example, one organization for which I served as a consultant introduced this kind of pay system to go with empowered teams. Subsequently many key senior employees became frustrated and demotivated, and in some cases left the company. Because the pay system especially rewarded new skill acquisition, junior-level employees, who had more to learn, were able to obtain greater pay increases. Consequently, the highly skilled senior employees became distracted from the commitment and psychological ownership they had been experiencing while the empowered team system was being rolled out. They developed a transactor outlook that led to feelings of inequity and alienation. A focus on pay had simply overshadowed their commitment and motivation.

In team-based work systems there are some real advantages to sharing rewards among all team members. That is, the best and the worst team members share the team's rewards. If someone is not contributing fully, the team works out a way to help that person improve. Sometimes teams carry struggling members for periods when they are facing some difficult personal problem. Team members often develop a camaraderie and an allegiance to each other. Rewards are still important to team members, but if they become the focus, the real advantages of teams—mutual support, cooperation, synergy—can be lost. Members frequently learn to get beyond concern about equity and genuinely celebrate the good fortunes of other team members.

Sometimes team members are not rewarded commensurate with their individual contributions. Some team members may be just a bit more skilled and tend to contribute more. Sometimes a team member is struggling with a physical or personal problem that temporarily holds back his or her ability to perform. Nevertheless, other rewards, such as the acceptance and support that members give to one another, often ultimately become more important to team members. When team members have established a supportive and cohesive environment on their team, it is hard not to think of them in terms of the old Boys Town slogan, "He's not heavy, he's my brother."

So does Jesus' story really suggest all these things directly? Perhaps not, but it does challenge us to reconsider the power of reinforcements, especially money, as the end-all of motivation. Maybe this alone is the important lesson that Jesus' story leaves us with. We shouldn't place undue focus on rewards that are separate from the task, the mission at hand. If we do, we will draw the attention away from more important questions such as, Are whole persons being encouraged to participate, including their creative thoughts, which could lead them to do something even better than we've asked them to do? Are we teaching people to be inspired, intelligent performers or comical trained miniature bears? Are we encouraging people to be committed or just compliant? Are we fostering a team attitude or a "What's in it for me?" attitude? Are we teaching people to celebrate the good fortune of their fellow human beings or to look out for number one?

WISE LEADERS FOSTER FOLLOWERS'
COMMITMENT AND TEAMWORK RATHER THAN
FOLLOWERS' CALCULATING COMPLIANCE

PART FOUR

PLANT GOLDEN MUSTARD SEEDS

Great trees grow from tiny seeds. Wise leadership involves planting good seeds in good places at the right times, and then letting great things grow.

PRACTICE MUSTARD SEED POWER

The kingdom of heaven is like a mustard seed that someone took and sowed in his field; it is the smallest of all the seeds, but when it has grown it is the greatest of shrubs and becomes a tree, so that the birds of the air come and make nests in its branches. (Matt. 13: 31–32)

I have always found this passage to be one of the most remarkable of all Jesus' teachings. Over the last few decades, especially in the west, our world has tended toward an ultra-fast pace and too often people, and the organizations they are connected to, have desired large quick payoffs. The pressure has been for ever-increasing sales, more profits, and larger returns on investments. Too often, the striving for more has been beyond reason . . . resulting in financial bubbles in technology and housing markets, and a host of accounting and financial debacles that nearly crippled the world economy. Sometimes everything has seemed to be exaggerated way beyond anything natural. It's almost as though we've been living in some kind of virtual-reality cartoon in which things are blown way out of proportion. If you want to survive in this sort of alternate reality, then a philosophy of "more is better" seems to rule the day. Don't do anything small; instead, exaggerate choices and actions no matter the costs.

This orientation, of course, poses significant implications for the practice of leadership. Leaders too often feel pressure to achieve dramatic results. Other times they simply have allowed themselves to be sucked into a desire for windfalls in wealth or power. Even when they do have sincerely good intentions, they can feel like they're supposed to be heroic figures who possess some kind of magical insight and charisma and that they should be dramatically leading the way for those they lead. And the people in their organizations respond to the expectations that they be dramatic as well. Some of these organizations aspire to become money factories that crank out huge profits and returns for their stockholders. Others may strive to be innovation factories that are always discovering giant breakthroughs or that try to reach absolutely optimum efficiency (which can mean cold, calculated management that pursues large cost reductions including cutting jobs to the bone) for the sake of squeezing out more financial returns. Much of this effort flows from human-created and human-perpetuated myths that we only infrequently realize are inconsistent with a more healthy and accurate view of reality.

To be fair, it's important to remember that many organizations had to make significant changes to meet the many challenges that have emerged in recent years. Some companies had become elaborate, wasteful bureaucracies that seemed to be set more on maintaining the status quo than on serving any useful purpose. And leadership was often sadly lacking within these rigid, rule-based structures. Instead, fanny-protecting management champions of resisting change, and consequently any kind of improvement, ruled the day. Thus many of the massive turbocharged changes that have invaded contemporary work and life have been welcomed as the dawning of a new, and hopefully better day. To some degree things had gotten so out of whack, so inefficient or unresponsive to the dynamics of the contemporary world that sometimes major (make that huge and thundering) changes were needed. Unfortunately, the human side of things may have been sacrificed in the new wave of change; the proverbial baby may be flying out the door with the bath water.

Jesus presents a deeply contrasting message. He seems to counsel that we don't have to worry about pursuing unrealistic larger-than-life illusions. Rather, the smallest of things—indeed, wee little mustard seeds—can be the source of great results. His message suggests that organizations and their leaders should think twice before they strive for the large, obvious choices, before they pull the ostentatious, shiny, loud-clanging action levers. Instead, the subtle, seemingly very small but positive and useful actions and things can be the real tickets to the greatest of results. As the ancient saying goes, "The journey of a thousand miles begins with a single step."

One of my favorite stories from classic business folklore that seems to illustrate this idea well is the now-famous 3M backdoor development of Post-it Notes. After the company had expended significant human and financial resources on a project, only to create a rather unsticky, inferior form of glue, one 3M-er discovered a simple, small way to use this failure. Putting the glue on little strips of paper, he found that he had created handy little markers that were useful as bookmarks in his hymnal as he sang in the church choir. He also found that they were handy for recording short notes. Later, after first marketing the discovery only internally to 3M employees, the positive response from other 3M-ers led to a whole new product. No grand technological innovation was involved—just a simple little idea addressing a very basic human activity—and it all resulted from what had appeared to be a failure. Of course the rest is history, as a focus on a small creative idea and not on large business and financial success ended up creating a virtual money tree that has netted 3M millions upon millions of dollars and enabled it to provide very practical assistance to countless people around the world.

Perhaps the 3M Post-it Note illustrates the lesson of mustard seed leadership. A more direct example that is probably closer to what Jesus was talking about is offered by the very popular book, *Random Acts of Kindness,*[1] a collection of stories, quotes, and ideas that suggest that each of us should look for opportunities to do the "do-able" little things that can help others and in the process contribute to a more positive world. Going out of our way to help someone with a troublesome problem, surprising someone with support and assistance when it's not called for or even deserved, and putting the needs of others ahead of our own all represent the spirit of this philosophy. Probably the best way to visualize the process is to picture that we are planting positive mustard seeds wherever we go. Imagine if a leader set out to plant as many of these potent little seeds as possible—each one offering the potential to produce rich, positive fruit. Instead of striving to act out some dramatic, charismatic role or achieve some large accomplishment on a stage that he or she feels compelled to dominate, the leader could concentrate on constructively spreading goodwill and serving as a positive model for others.

According to this view, leaders do not need to be charismatic headline grabbers, nor do their followers. Two particular forms of leadership have repeatedly marked both famous and infamous leaders throughout history. These leadership types have been described elsewhere and have been called *strongman* and *visionary hero* leadership.[2] Strongman leadership is an autocratic approach to influencing others that is based primarily on fear and intimidation. Many ruthless international dictators, intimidating sports coaches, and hard-nosed business leaders have adopted this strategy. It tends to result in fear-based compliance. Followers do what leaders command as long as the leaders are around to wield their power. If the leaders leave, or are somehow reduced to a weakened position, followers are usually ready and anxious to help with and celebrate their downfall.

Conversely, visionary heroes, which I discussed in the chapter on committing to ethical behavior, appear to be far more appealing and positive. In fact, in times of crisis or major change, visionary heroes are often the most needed type of leader. But the spotlight tends to be dominated by these often charismatic influencers. Followers are usually committed to the leader or to his or her cause, but they also tend to be dependent on the leader. If the leader leaves or is somehow removed, the movement tends to collapse, because the leader has become a single pillar of strength that is suddenly torn from under the entire structure. I noted earlier that many people commonly regarded as great leaders displayed a visionary hero style, including Gandhi, Martin Luther King, Jr., and John F. Kennedy. Because of the dominant central focus on the leader, this approach also poses the risk of leading followers to disaster or to very unethical ends. Adolf Hitler, Jim Jones, and David

Koresh, among others, served as visionary heroes of doom for their followers.

Perhaps the key point of Jesus' lesson of the mustard seed is to remember that we are, after all, limited human beings. As such we don't have to strive for dramatic effect. Rather, if we try our best and concentrate on the little positive things we accomplish each day, great things may well emerge. William Blake put it well: "To see a world in a grain of sand and a heaven in a wild flower,/Hold infinity in the palm of your hand and eternity in an hour." Jesus tells us to be aware of the power in little things. Indeed, planting even the smallest of seeds, a mustard seed, if it is positively alive and planted well, can lead to a great result.

WISE LEADERS UNDERSTAND THE

POWER OF SMALL THINGS THAT CAN BE

THE SEEDS OF GREATNESS

LEAD WITH THE POWER OF GOLDEN MUSTARD SEEDS

If you have faith the size of a mustard seed, you will say to this mountain, "Move from here to there," and it will move; and nothing will be impossible for you. (Matt. 17: 20–21)

The remarkable potential of the kind of leadership Jesus suggests is most powerfully described in this passage from his teachings. The central driving force is faith—a concept that Jesus talked about repeatedly in his teachings. Jesus suggests that if we have just the smallest amount of faith—the size of only a mustard seed—nothing will be impossible for us. A rather bold statement this is indeed.

It is remarkable how many men and women throughout history seemingly defied the impossible when armed with belief and determination. Roger Banister accomplished what was believed to be impossible—he ran a mile in less than four minutes. A few years later, armed with the belief that it could be done, dozens of runners were doing it. Thomas Edison achieved the seemingly impossible over and over: he enabled light to be produced in a hollow tube of glass, recorded the human voice on a piece of plastic, invented pictures that show life in full motion, and made many other miraculous discoveries. The Wright brothers discovered a device to enable humans to fly like birds. Indeed, the list of miracles accomplished by mortal human beings lacking any unusual or superhuman advantages goes on and on. Some would say that these people were armed with faith alone.

Of course the faith Jesus referred to is belief and trust in God. He was talking about a spiritual allegiance and a source of strength that is beyond human ability. This is indeed a fork in the road for many of us. I am especially conscious of this after serving many years as a college professor. In academia, empirical facts often rule supreme. This generally requires that we have some objective and observable basis for recording and measuring the phenomena we study. The idea of having faith in something we cannot touch, see, or measure does not sit particularly well with many academics; we simply are not trained to accept such fuzzy ideas. Many of us place limits on what we will acknowledge as being real. We force the world to conform to our limitations. To do otherwise would require us to admit openly and embrace the fact that we ourselves are vastly limited—an act of humility, courage, and, yes, faith that many are either unwilling or unable to accept.

Nevertheless, at the outset I said that this book was not intended to be a religious work. I stated that I intended to focus on the practical wisdom that can be gleaned from Jesus' teachings in order to provide insight on effective ways to lead ourselves and others. In that spirit I will not enter into an in-depth analysis of the religious underpinnings and implications of the lessons that Jesus taught. Suffice it to say that this analysis of these lessons provides an incomplete view—a view that limits our understanding to the more concrete principles that can be reasonably digested relative to human experience.

At the same time, the lesson of this chapter pulls precariously close to falling outside this domain. Jesus said that with faith we could move mountains, we could do anything. This is a powerful proclamation based on a powerful idea—faith. Even within the domain of reasonable human experience, the power of belief has been demonstrated repeatedly, as has been illustrated in these chapters. The practical lesson—do not underestimate the power of what you believe—is highly potent. As Mark Twain reportedly put it, "If you think you can, or you think you can't, you're probably right."

This kind of perspective is demonstrated in both the achievement and philosophy expressed by former corporate executive and recent Republican candidate for senator of California, Carly Fiorina.[1] In 1999 she was appointed President and CEO of Hewlett-Packard (HP). Despite later running into difficulties that led to her leaving the company, her appointment at HP made her, among all woman top executives in history, the one leading the largest enterprise ever. Regardless of political leanings or business philosophy, it is difficult to not be impressed by what Fiorina has done with her life. In a personal interview she said "... I grew up with [a feeling that has carried over] into my life and my professional career ... a sense of 'no limitations.' I grew up in a family where my parents made it very clear that I could do anything I wanted to do, and the only limitation that was placed on me was the one I put on myself."[2] This spirit of exceptional belief, and a sense of mustard seed power, is apparent in views she has shared about leadership. In her words, "Every man and every woman on this earth is born to lead. A leader's greatest obligation is to make possible an environment where people's minds and hearts can be inventive, brave ... where people can aspire to change the world ... I love ... seeing people and seeing organizations do more than they thought they were capable of. I just love to see it."[3]

It is also very important to keep the Golden Rule in mind. Jesus frequently advocated his own version of this rule, either directly or indirectly, throughout his teaching. The idea is to use the power of faith (belief), but also to focus it on something worthwhile (a sincere concern for the welfare of others). That is, we can have potentially mountain-moving golden mustard seed power if we faithfully pursue doing for others as we would have them do for us. Indeed, Jesus' teachings point to no greater way for humans to wield constructive power than by combining the Golden Rule with the planting of positive mustard seeds in human hearts.

One of the most poignant examples of this kind of mountain-moving behavior was demonstrated through the caring leadership style of business folk hero Aaron Feuerstein, which was touched on briefly earlier in this book. In 1995, much of Feuerstein's textile company in Lawrence, Massachusetts, was destroyed by a huge fire. Despite the devastation left in the wake of the conflagration, he refused to follow the advice of many to close down his mills. Instead, he kept all of his 2,400 employees on payroll, costing him $1.5 million a week and risking his entire life's savings in the process. The board of directors, executives, and his family thought he was crazy, but he felt an obligation to his workforce. He also refused to be the one to "kill" the town of Lawrence, which depended so heavily on his company as the primary source of employment for its residents that it would have been all but destroyed if he shut down. He simply put the welfare of others ahead of himself.

The mustard seeds he planted grew into large trees indeed. Weekly production of the mill's Polartec fabric went up more than 50 percent compared to output before the fire. Feuerstein proclaimed, "They have paid me back nearly tenfold." And he openly advocated the compassionate kind of leadership that he has so admirably demonstrated: "We must show workers the kind of loyalty they extend to us.... Not in the short term, but in the long term, when companies act in an ethical way, it's good for business and good for the shareholder."[4]

Feuerstein reported that he received nearly ten thousand letters from employees across the country. Many stated that his actions restored their faith, which had been badly shaken by the vast number of companies whose cold, calculated approach to business had left them feeling that organization leaders no longer care about their employees. They viewed Malden Mills as a symbol of what they would like to see in corporate America. Feuerstein argued that businesses can be run successfully without focusing only on the bottom line and without caving in to pressures to downsize, but few try it. He closed his comments during a 1997 presentation to the Economic Club of Phoenix with a quote from the prophet Jeremiah and then added his own related advice to focus on kindness and justice instead of wealth: "Let the modern-day CEO not brag about stock options...but of social responsibility and charity they have shown to workers and their community."

However, the story, and the challenges, of Malden Mills does not end here. Limitations in the insurance settlement for rebuilding the factory, a declining economy, other firms making less expensive knockoffs of Polartec fabric, and various other pressures in the industry that forced dozens of textile plants like Malden Mills to shut down, eventually forced Feuerstein to file for Chapter 11.[5] Nevertheless, even in the face of this seemingly hopeless setback, he never gave up hope of saving the jobs of his 1,200 employees and committed himself to bringing the firm back to profitability and emerging from bankruptcy. In late 2003, the firm did just that and later, Congress approved a multimillion dollar expenditure for Polartec garments for all branches of the U.S. military. This, combined with a $100-million sale of land adjacent to Malden Mills to a real-estate developer, enabled Feuerstein to keep the company, and the jobs it provided, alive for a few more years. More recently the company faced further financial woes and became a newly named company called Polartec (the name of its signature product). Regardless of the end of the story, Aaron Feuerstein is cemented in business history (and his legacy lives on in the hearts of the thousands of workers to whom he gave hope) for his demonstration of how a leader, relying on the power of faith and a firm commitment to the welfare of others, can stand up to even the most formidable setbacks and challenges and plant potent seeds for the future.

In the end, when challenged to boil down his philosophy to its essence, Jesus was very candid and direct.

*And one of them, a lawyer, asked him a question to test him.
"Teacher, which commandment in the law is the greatest?"
He said to him, "You shall love the Lord your God with all
your heart, and with all your soul, and with all your mind.
This is the greatest and first commandment. And a second is
like it: You shall love your neighbor as yourself. On these two
commandments hang all the law and the prophets."* (Matt.
22: 35–40)

In this simple statement, Jesus made his idea of the ultimate goal clear—he set the sights squarely on love.

The lesson of golden mustard seed power suggests that love mixed with faith (the power of belief) can be the ultimate source of strength. This is especially notable for leaders, who are continually confronted with choices about how they will treat and influence others. Jesus suggests that the combination of love and faith is far more potent than mixing nitro and glycerin or any other explosive combination. Maybe someday these two powerful elements will be widely embraced as the ultimate sources of truly great leadership. To date, only a small number of leaders, like Gandhi and Mother Teresa and apparently Aaron Feuerstein, seem to have understood this. Maybe that is the ultimate lesson Jesus' teachings will continue to offer leaders, today and for millennia to come: lead with love and faith (with golden mustard seed power), and overcoming mountainous challenges, indeed accomplishing almost anything worthwhile, will be possible.

LOVE AND FAITH ARE THE

ULTIMATE INGREDIENTS FOR

MOUNTAIN-MOVING LEADERSHIP

DON'T TRY TO SERVE TWO MASTERS

No one can serve two masters; for a slave will either hate the one and love the other, or be devoted to the one and despise the other. You cannot serve God and wealth. (Matt. 6: 24)

Jesus was unsurpassed in raising the most important and the most challenging issues in life. This verse typifies this style. It challenges all of us to deeply consider our life purpose (you might prefer the word "mission" if you think in those terms); perhaps especially those who want to live a positive meaningful life but who also possess ambition and desire "to get ahead."

In fact, the first edition of *The Leadership Wisdom of Jesus* evoked a frequent response from readers. It went something like this: "The book was very helpful to me and supported much of what I believe and wish was more common in the workplace. However, how can you reconcile Jesus' emphasis on ideals such as compassion and honesty with the hard realities of the tough competitive business world?" Or, in other words, how do fundamental business values focused on profitability, efficiency, and accountability fit with the virtues that Jesus taught such as love, forgiveness, and integrity?

As I thought about the second edition of this book and what I might add, it was this sticky area that kept coming to mind. I must confess that it was with some hesitation that I finally concluded that a chapter focused on the clash—and hopefully the potential synergy—between traditional business values and spiritual virtues would be right on target. Again, I want to preface my comments by reminding readers, and myself, that I am not a theologian and I am not trying to convert others or to impose some kind of spiritual agenda on anyone. However, I do think this chapter raises important questions that I believe are crucial for us all to consider in our quest for more effective leadership of ourselves and others. I also think such a discussion is particularly timely when considering that company names like Enron, WorldCom, and Tyco have received so much attention concerning their infamous business scandals, that they have all but become clichés. Add to that other monumental ethical failings worthy of membership in a virtual Hall of Shame, like the major abuses that occurred in the mortgage industry, causing a housing market collapse, and Bernie Madoff's infamous Ponzi scheme, and it quickly becomes apparent that the wise lesson of Jesus introduced in this chapter is very timely indeed.

Sad images of executives abusing power and misrepresenting financial results are still fresh in the minds of many people. Ultimately, at Enron, and other firms, bankruptcy followed. And more importantly, thousands of workers lost their life's savings as a result. While mental images remain of greedy managers operating from lavish executive suites, misusing power to manipulate organizations (and the people that work for and depend on them) for personal gain, it is refreshing to see other executives who have chosen a far different path. CEO Aaron Feuerstein, mentioned more than once elsewhere in this book, showed compassion and courage when he risked all of his personal wealth by continuing to pay his workforce while his company was being rebuilt in the wake of a catastrophic fire. He was a successful businessman who put his neck on the line for others, seemingly in contradiction to "good business sense." And I get a kick personally out of the image of former CEO (and more recently a political candidate) Meg Whitman, having held several prestigious positions, with all their executive trappings at the likes of Procter & Gamble, Disney, and Hasbro/Playskool, agreeing to lead then-fledgling eBay. Under her leadership, eBay became a multibillion-dollar sales powerhouse, and she led the company from a humble cubicle, much like the ones that other employees at the company worked from.[1] I also think of Dean Cycon, founder and CEO of Dean's Beans (previously described in the chapter "Let Your Light Shine"). He has prioritized social and environmental values over profit to the point that he actually traveled to the small villages and stayed in the huts of the indigenous coffee growers from whom he purchased coffee beans, intentionally at above market prices.

Despite these contrasting examples, all too often it seems that we mostly just read about power-hungry executive leaders out for personal gain. Traditional business values, such as profit, efficiency, and rationality, have dominated the literature on organizations relative to concepts related to virtues such as compassion and caring. For example, in a study of articles appearing in the *Wall Street Journal*, words focused on things like "winning" and "competitive advantage" were being used at an increasing rate while concepts such as virtue and caring were nearly nonexistent.[2] Yet dominant business values that focus on the bottom line may directly contradict an individual's deep personal and even spiritual beliefs. When individuals have values such as integrity and honesty, but work in organizations emphasizing a ruthless pursuit of profitability, they may experience significant personal pressure to behave in uncaring and even unethical ways.

Unfortunately, recent history has demonstrated that individuals sometimes act in ways that are consistent with group or organization norms but directly contradict their personal values and beliefs. In fact, Enron-type scandals can be perpetuated by otherwise caring and honest people setting aside their deeper personal values and either engaging in or condoning harmful, immoral, or illegal behavior. In order to fulfill work roles or to comply with directives from superiors, the kind of lessons Jesus taught sometimes are thrown out the window in favor of getting ahead or avoiding risking job security.

Jesus' teachings, on the other hand, challenge us to stay the course and answer the call to a more virtuous life and career. We are challenged to pursue the very best in ourselves and follow a path that may not offer quick riches, power, and career advancement but rather offers the potential for a vital and flourishing life, filled with deeper meaning and purpose.

Carol Tome, the Chief Financial Officer (CFO) of Home Depot as well as chair of the Atlanta Federal Reserve Board and only the second woman in over 150 years appointed as Chair of the Metro Atlanta Chamber of Commerce, shared an interesting personal experience with having temporarily lost her focus on what was most important.[3] She told of how when she first held a leadership position, she gave a performance appraisal to someone over the phone because she was more focused on financial and business success than the value of the person. She explained, "That was terrible, not a very thoughtful thing to do. The reason I did it over the phone was that I was involved in a deal, and I made that more important than meeting with this associate." Consequently, the associate left the firm and Tome realized it was because of her. She still regrets not having taken the time to meet with the person, "To this day I kick myself for that." She added, "my mother instilled in me a deep moral compass, driven by faith in God as well as how important it is to give back . . ." Later she described how her perspective about work has changed to serve her deeper beliefs better. She still puts in the effort for business success but that is not the primary focus ("the master") that she values most. She emphasized the point by reflecting on what her tombstone might read: "If it read, 'She worked hard,' that would mean I had failed. If it read, 'She made a difference in my life,' it would mean I had succeeded."

The foundation for committing to a life that includes the pursuit of virtue, even in highly competitive environments, is probably strongest when established early. Coach Clayton Kendrick-Holmes has tried to do just that for the young men thatwho have played football for him at Maritime College. The Department of athletics statement of Vision, Mission, Purposes and Guiding Principles emphasizes a variety of higher level values (virtues) such as responsibility, integrity, respect, courtesy, loyalty, and trust. And under Kendrick-Holmes, the football team has gone so far as to put such virtues—respect, responsibility, and character—on the back of their alternate home jerseys in place of players' names to remind team members of what they are playing for. The team has received significant recognition for its winning record and various accomplishments (including placing the most players of any team on the Eastern Collegiate Football Conference Team in 2009 and achieving a perfect ten wins and no losses record in 2010). And Coach

Kendrick-Holmes was recently named Coach of the Year for D3Football.com East Region, American Football Coaches Association (AFCA) Region 1, and the Eastern Collegiate Football Conference. Yet perhaps what stands out the most, is the coach's and team's emphasis on being good persons committed to virtue beyond just being competitive. It's fascinating to think about what might happen if something similar occurred in the competitive world of business. Imagine, business executives taking a similar stand by putting values on their business cards (e.g., integrity, honesty, compassion) instead of impressive sounding titles, to remind themselves and others what they value most and are really working towards.

The lessons taught by Jesus challenge each of us to make a strong commitment to more virtuous values such as compassion, honesty, and integrity even when they, at least in the short run, contradict business values.[4] For example, this might mean choosing to provide a compassionate demeanor and extra service to a customer with special needs even though the company norm is to handle such customer problems with an efficient cost-effective yet uncaring response. Or, it might call for fully supporting a legal or ethical standard, such as creating optimum safety in the manufacturing of a product or providing a service, even in the face of organizational pressure to accomplish work in an efficient, low-cost manner that compromises safety standards.

Leading according to a higher standard requires these kinds of difficult choices. It also demands careful attention to the kind of people we select and develop to surround us when we are in a position of leadership. It can be very tempting to select only people who agree with and support our ideas, and whose loyalty overshadows other values. Yet, in the complex, dynamic, global business environment leaders face today, it is of utmost importance to work with people who will hold us accountable and challenge us if we begin wandering into ethically murky areas. This points to a new kind of loyalty that supports leaders to be virtuous and not just successful in a traditional business sense. Jesus' teachings about compassion and forgiveness in no way rule out the importance of accountability and, in fact, reinforce its importance. But this accountability extends to leaders as much or more than their followers and it calls for standards based on virtues such as compassion, integrity, wisdom, and courage to do the right thing, and not just measures of profitability and business success.

It is also important to emphasize that it is possible for success in business (in terms of profitability and overall financial return) and choosing virtuous actions, to complement each other... they do not have to be diametrically opposed. For example, Sir John Templeton, arguably one of the most successful investors in history, enjoyed spectacular financial success in business, punctuated by his founding of the extremely profitable Templeton Mutual Funds. Yet, throughout his business career, he believed that spiritual principles and values, not business ones, are the most important. He even relied on spirituality and prayer to guide his business decisions.

In fact, originally, Templeton wanted to be a missionary but realized that his talents were greater in business and that many others had more talent for missionary work. Consequently he decided that he could do more good by pursuing a business career that would enable him to generate the resources needed to support missionaries and other workers involved directly in spiritual pursuits. Templeton believed in the oneness of humankind and managed the Templeton funds with a focus beyond himself as a way of serving others, both his clients and the many spiritual workers that were providing service to the world. Today he has literally changed the world through the Templeton Foundation (which provides millions of dollars in funding for projects serving humankind across the globe) and the Templeton Prize, the largest philanthropic monetary award in existence.

His inspiring example raises the importance of means–end relationships—keeping clear what are our ends and what means are available to help us reach them. Business financial success can be a means for serving humankind. Consistent with Jesus' teachings, Templeton did not *serve two masters... God and wealth*. Rather, he worked diligently and ethically in his business pursuits as a way of serving God and the people on the planet who he viewed as his brothers and sisters. Despite the difficult challenge seemingly posed by the tension between spiritual values and career success, people like Templeton introduce a new sense of hopefulness. Talents applied well with integrity, compassion and wisdom can provide a foundation for servant leadership if we can keep straight which "master" we are ultimately serving.

EXAMINE YOUR REFLECTION

Take a moment to do a quick review of some of the lessons Jesus taught. The passages below are excerpts from many of the scripture lesssons that were introduced at the beginning of chapters throughout this book.

Consider the larger image about leadership that arises from just a few of the many surprising, often counterintuitive, and wise things that Jesus said.

- *... take the log out of your own eye, and then you will see clearly to take the speck out of your neighbor's eye.*

- *Whoever wants to be first must be last of all and servant of all.*

- *... do not worry about tomorrow ... today's trouble is enough for today.*

- *You are the light of the world ... let your light shine ...*

- *Let anyone among you who is without sin be the first to throw a stone ...*

- *... love your enemies and pray for those who persecute you ...*

- *In everything do to others as you would have them do to you.*

- *Do not judge and you will not be judged ... forgive and you will be forgiven; give, and it will be given to you ...*

- *...a mustard seed... is the smallest of all seeds, but when it has grown it is the greatest of all shrubs and becomes a tree...*

- *If you have faith the size of a mustard seed, you will say to this mountain, "Move from here to there," and it will move... nothing will be impossible for you.*

What relevance do these lessons have for you? To what extent do these teachings of Jesus reflect your own personal philosophy, belief system, and behavior? Do you lead yourself with the leadership wisdom of Jesus? When you are in a position of leadership for others, do you lead with the leadership wisdom of Jesus? Would you like to embrace these lessons more in your life and work?

The purpose of this chapter is to provide you with an opportunity to look in the mirror... to gain understanding of yourself through some self-reflection. First, a short questionnaire is provided for you to engage in some self-assessment regarding where your thinking is right now. Instructions for interpreting your responses to the questionnaire are provided as well. Then some work and life scenarios are provided so that you can further reflect on your personal leadership beliefs and tendencies. Each scenario will afford a chance for you to consider how you would handle the challenges involved... to look in a metaphorical mirror from different angles.

At the outset I want to make clear that the material in this chapter was not created for the purpose of scientific investigation. The questionnaire and scenarios for personal reflection were not designed with rigorous psychometric properties in mind for obtaining reliability and validity of responses across a subject population for research purposes. Rather, the items in the questionnaire and the situational descriptions that follow were written for the purpose of facilitating personal reflection and insight. Think of this chapter as an opportunity, now that you have read the content of this book, to reflect and take stock concerning the relationship of Jesus' Leadership Wisdom to how you are living, both in your work and personal life. While some of the questions and scenarios zero in on personal and potentially value-loaded issues, keep in mind that your responses are private and designed for your own self-insight. So, being thoughtful and honest with yourself regarding your responses should provide you with the most benefit.

Let's get started. Begin by responding to the following questionnaire.

Leadership Wisdom of Jesus Questionnaire (LWJQ)

Respond to the following twenty statements (you can write your response next to each item or on a separate piece of paper). Choose a number 1 to 5:

1 = Does not describe me at all
2 = Does not describe me very well
3 = Describes me somewhat
4 = Describes me well
5 = Describes me very well

for each statement corresponding with the description that best describes your view. Try your best to be brutally honest with yourself concerning your responses so that you can gain the most accurate and helpful insights about your current perspective.

1. When I act as a leader, it is more important that I lead myself and get my own act together than that I critically evaluate others.

2. I try to put the spotlight on others rather than seeking recognition for myself.

3. It is more important to me that I have good internal values as a basis for my actions than that I act in ways that others will approve of.

4. I am able to avoid worrying most of the time, even when I face significant difficulties.

5. I commit to doing what is right without rationalizing ethical compromises.

6. Whenever I am in a position of leadership, I try to model in my own behavior what I think is right.

7. I am able to avoid self-righteous judgment when others fail because I recognize my own human limitations.

8. I choose to try to express love and support for everyone, even my opponents and enemies, to the best of my ability.

9. I live and lead by the golden rule... I treat others as I would have them treat me.

10. I let go of judgmental feelings when I feel them arise toward people or situations.

11. I view and treat everyone as having unique value.

12. When I promote change, I do my best to communicate with and support those that will be affected, before the changes take place.

13. I view mistakes and failures of others more as an opportunity for learning than as occasions for judgment and punishment.

14. I believe that the most effective leaders tend to spend more time supporting and serving others than wielding power to influence people to do what the leaders want.

15. I try to make sure that I, and those I lead, help each other see clearly where we are trying to go.

16. To me, real achievement has less to do with a person's absolute level of performance and more with contributing to her/his full potential.

17. I would rather have people commit (go above and beyond) in their own way than comply (do what I ask and no more) with my way of doing things.

18. I believe that even modest accomplishments can plant seeds for significant later changes if they are pursued with the right spirit and intent.

19. I believe in the vast potential of myself and those I lead and maintain the view that we can accomplish great things.

20. Staying true to higher-level values such as compassion and integrity are at least as important to me as achieving wealth and success.

Interpreting Your Score

Add up the numbers you chose for each of the twenty statements. Your total should be somewhere in a range between 20–100. Keep in mind that responses to questionnaires are only as accurate as the clarity and veracity with which a person responds, and may vary based on current mood or outlook. Nevertheless, the higher your score the more it suggests that your thinking tendencies at this time (at least as captured by this self-assessment questionnaire) are consistent with *The Leadership Wisdom of Jesus* lessons addressed in this book. Using a simple proportional mathematical breakdown for each possible range of responses (from lowest possible numerical response to highest possible response), a rough interpretation of possible scores is listed below:

A score of 20–36 suggests a very low level of consistency with the lessons in this book.

A score of 37–52 suggests a low level of consistency with the lessons in this book.

A score of 53–68 suggests a moderate level of consistency with the lessons in this book.

A score of 69–84 suggests a high level of consistency with the lessons in this book.

A score of 85–100 suggests a very high level of consistency with the lessons in this book.

Regardless of how you responded and what your total score was, the primary value in this exercise is in the self-reflection it encourages. In fact, you can ignore your score altogether if you like — it is just a rough overall indicator and useful only to the extent that you find it helpful. What's important is your thinking relative to each of the statements on the questionnaire which are based on the chapter lessons offered throughout the book. By reflecting on each of the statements and the extent to which you see them as consistent with your own point of view and action tendencies you have begun to consider how well the specific lessons in this book apply to you at this point in your life. To further encourage this process the next section offers some situations for you to think about and an opportunity to consider how you might respond to each.

Leadership Scenarios for Personal Reflection

The following are sample incidents for personal reflection. These kinds of situational descriptions, and others that you may think of, can be useful for doing some self-examination and thinking about your beliefs and response tendencies when faced by real life scenarios. They can also be used for promoting group discussion and development in learning or reading groups.

Read the following examples of challenging situations of self-leadership and leadership-of-others and consider how you would respond. Briefly write down your thoughts about each situation in the space provided (use another sheet of paper, your laptop, or other note-taking device to record more of your thoughts if you need more room).

1. During a trip, you go into a carry-out restaurant that is advertising sandwiches on special for $5. After ordering your sandwich, for some reason you are charged $6.75 rather than $5. When you inquire about this, the employee behind the counter explains the reason for the higher price but the line of customers is long and the restaurant is busy and loud, so you don't hear clearly what he says.

You decide to let it go. Later, however, you realize that the waiter also charged you for a drink even though you didn't purchase one, and it is too late to go back to the restaurant. The next day you eat at another restaurant and you realize your wait person has filled out your bill in a way that charges you $1.50 less than you actually owe. Do you say something or do you consider this simply another restaurant billing mistake that will help even out the overcharge from the day before?

2. While at work, your boss criticizes you for making a fairly minor mistake on a project that you have worked very hard on and that you believe you have performed quite well on overall. A short while later, one of your direct reports makes a mistake. You know this worker has been working hard, feels bad about the mistake, and seems intent on not doing it again. You also realize that, given his experience, the mistake should not have been made. Would you focus more on criticizing him and letting him know that you disapprove (as your boss did with you) or would you focus more on expressing your appreciation of his hard work and emphasize the learning that can be gained from the error?

3. You notice in the news a report that your organization has made a large profit recently. You also note that many of your peers have been using company supplies and other resources for their own personal use. Given the recent large financial returns enjoyed by your organization, would you be inclined to do the same, given that your efforts helped create the recent profits?

4. You are a leader in a department where some members have been making particularly significant contributions (in terms of output or sales). You also have a new employee who has been trying hard and making gradual performance improvements, but whose contributions have been comparatively minor. Would you focus your appreciation and recognition on your high-performers, giving relatively little recognition and attention to your new employee? Or, would you make it a point to take time to encourage the new employee and acknowledge the effort and progress she has been making?

5. As a leader, you have noted that certain types of changes and innovations you facilitate (such as those focused on your star employees) tend to produce large payoffs fairly quickly. On the other hand, some other more modest efforts that don't yield large results in the short run, tend to plant the seeds for significant results later (such as working with younger less experienced workers). Would you tend to focus your efforts on things that pay off in a big way now or would you take the time to focus on things that yield more modest immediate outcomes but plant the seeds for larger returns in the future?

6. You work for an organization with members who hold widely varying attitudes about what the firm can potentially accomplish, ranging from highly optimistic to more pessimistic (what some describe as being "realistic"). Some of your colleagues think your company and the people in it can literally change the world—making great innovative discoveries and providing products and services that can do much good. Yet others tend to scoff at these "unrealistic optimists." Instead, they take a position that, given economic and other pressures, and the inherent limitations of human beings and their organization, little of significance will ever really be accomplished.

Which of these viewpoints would you be more likely to lean towards?

Conclusion

This chapter was intended to provide a mirror of sorts. Hopefully, considering the statements in the questionnaire (and how well you believe they apply to you), as well as how you might respond to the scenarios that followed, gave you a beginning look, even if only a blurry one, at your mirror image relative to the lessons in this book. Indeed, Jesus taught many lessons, the wisdom of which can only be appreciated with deep and continued reflection. I know my observations of myself and others when faced with challenges that require wise leadership, all too often seem to fall well short. Perhaps this is all part of the amazing journey of being alive in such interesting and challenging times. Someone who spends more time forgiving than judging, serving than being served, empowering than controlling, honoring than being honored, appreciating than criticizing, loving than hating, and believing in what's possible than declaring what's impossible, are among the many wise leadership characteristics Jesus seems to want us to see... when we look in the mirror.

MORE FORGIVING THAN JUDGING,

SERVING THAN BEING SERVED,

EMPOWERING THAN CONTROLLING,

HONORING THAN BEING HONORED,

APPRECIATING THAN CRITICIZING,

LOVING THAN HATING,

AND BELIEVING IN WHAT'S POSSIBLE

THAN DECLARING WHAT'S

IMPOSSIBLE... LEADERSHIP WISDOM OF JESUS

TO LOOK FOR IN THE MIRROR

THE LEADERSHIP WISDOM OF JESUS

THIRD EDITION

In the months and years following the original publication of *The Leadership Wisdom of Jesus,* I learned that many reading groups and classes used the book as a resource for discussion. These groups met in a variety of contexts such as college classrooms, adult church classes, business executive groups, men's groups, and so forth, both in the U.S. and abroad. Sometimes I was asked to speak at conferences or gatherings but most often the groups met on their own. On occasion I was asked for suggestions to help the groups with their study and discussions. Here I will share some brief thoughts about the kinds of things I have suggested to groups for consideration when they used the book. I will divide my advice into three primary parts. First, I will make suggestions on how the new chapter in this third edition—"Examine Your Reflection"—can be used to support group exploration and discussion of the various lessons included in this book. Second, a series of questions are offered to help in preparations for convening a reading group that is tailored to the needs of the participants. Third, a number of discussion questions are offered to provide some initial points for discussion among group members.

Keep in mind that I tried to write the book so that it could serve as a personal resource and point of reflection for a variety of contexts and for people from varied backgrounds. Also remember, as I have tried to make very clear, I am not a minister or theologian. Rather, I wear several other hats including that of a professor, consultant and speaker, husband and parent, writer, and a veteran of a variety of work settings and life experiences and challenges. I believe the key to having a successful discussion group is to carefully consider the specific needs and interests of the members of your group.

Obviously the nature and tone of your meetings will differ significantly depending on the context—for example, if they take place at someone's home as a neighborhood reading group, or in a business organization, or in a church or other religious setting.

Suggestions Based on the Chapter
"Examine Your Reflection"

At the outset I want to emphasize that the previous chapter titled "Examine Your Reflection" is intended to provide significant new material for assisting individual readers and groups in thinking about *The Leadership Wisdom of Jesus* lessons addressed in this book. I encourage readers to draw from that chapter, pulling questions and scenarios that are found to be especially relevant for a reading group, to support and encourage group discussion and reflection. More specifically I offer the following suggestions.

1. Encourage discussion group members to read and respond to the self-assessment questionnaire (preferably prior to a group meeting). Discuss the scores of the various individuals in the group (of course, allow for the possibility of some members preferring that their scores remain confidential) and what insights they gained from responding to the questionnaire.

2. Allow members to comment on the extent to which items on the questionnaire hit a chord with them—did the statements seem relevant to their own life and work experience? Were any of the items particularly helpful to reflect on? Did any of the items get under the skin of group members, triggering feelings of defensiveness or

criticalness about seeming naiveté or unfair standards that the items implied, given the realities of life and work?

3. Facilitate discussion about the scenarios offered in the chapter. Did members of the group especially identify or connect with a particular scenario? Consider focusing in on a scenario that a number of members of the discussion group found of particular interest. Ask the group if they can think of other challenging situations beyond the scenarios offered in the chapter.

4. Discuss where group members, having responded to the questionnaire and considered the scenarios, see themselves overall in terms of *The Leadership Wisdom of Jesus* . . . in their lives? . . . in their work? Would participants like to increase the relevance and adoption of *The Leadership Wisdom* in their behavior in life and work? How might the lessons offered in the book be increased going forward?

5. Discuss other reactions or thoughts generated by the chapter for various group members. If raising this general invitation to the group does not generate a response, consider singling out specific items from the questionnaire or specific scenarios for more in-depth group discussion.

A) For example, you might facilitate discussion around specific items of the questionnaire such as:

• I commit to doing what is right without rationalizing ethical compromises.

• I am able to avoid self-righteous judgment when others fail because I recognize my own human limitations.

- I choose to try to express love and support for everyone, even my opponents and enemies, to the best of my ability.

- What reactions do these statements cause for group members? Do they seem like realistic ideals to strive toward? What are some of the challenges that might be encountered in trying to embody these kinds of principles in our self-leadership or leadership of others in the world today?

B) Raise a scenario from the chapter for group discussion such as the following one:

You are a leader of a department where some members have been making particularly significant contributions (in terms of output or sales). You also have a new employee who has been trying hard and making gradual performance improvements, but whose contributions have been comparatively minor. Would you focus your appreciation and recognition on your high-performers, giving relatively little recognition and attention to your new employee? Or, would you make it a point to take time to encourage the new employee and acknowledge the effort and progress she has been making?

What kind of responses does this scenario generate from the group? Ask for specific reactions. Does the scenario reflect the experience of any of the members of the group? If such a situation has been encountered by one or more group members how was it handled and what were the results?

Questions to Consider Before Convening
a Group or Class

As mentioned above, the success of a discussion group is
significantly affected by the extent that specific needs and
interests of members are addressed. Different types of groups
—community, business, church, educational classes, etc.—will
likely require a different kind of focus and tone. With this in
mind I suggest that you think about the following questions
before convening your group:

1. What is the purpose of our group? Why are participants
   involved and what do they hope to learn and gain from
   their involvement?

2. What kinds of language and nature of discussion will
   be most inclusive and effective for the members of the
   group? For example, is more religious language consistent
   with the makeup of the group and something that will
   draw people in and help them to more effectively connect
   with the discussion or will it create a spirit of resistance in
   some members?

3. Are the group members equal peers or do authority structures or status issues need to be considered (for example,
   do certain members report to other members in the group
   as part of their work role)?

4. Is the context of this group public (such as a state university or community group that receives funding support
   from the state, city or federal government) or private
   (such as a private college or voluntary membership-based
   club)?

5. What other considerations can you think of that might help you decide how best to create a context of open, inclusive communication, or whatever else is most consistent with the needs and goals of the participants?

Another important part of creating a successful discussion group or class centers on the kinds of specific ideas and topics that are addressed. Some classes have reviewed and discussed the book sequentially on a simple chapter-by-chapter basis. Others have approached the book with a specific theme in mind such as "exploring how to become an effective *servant leader.*" As an example of how servant leadership might be taught and discussed in a learning context, a colleague of mine has used the book, and especially the chapter "Lead by Serving," as background material and then taken a number of passages from the scriptures that directly address the idea of being a servant as a basis for discussion. Some of the specific verses include:

> *. . . whoever wishes to become great among you must be your servant and whoever wishes to be first among you must become the slave of all.* (Mark 10: 44)

> *So if I, your Lord and Teacher, have washed your feet, you ought to wash one another's feet. For I have set you an example, that you also should do as I have done to you.* (John 13: 14–15)

> *No one has greater love than this, to lay down one's life for one's friends. You are my friends if you do what I command you. I do not call you servants any longer, because the servant does not know what the master is doing; but I have called you friends . . .* (John 15: 13–15)

By reflecting on and discussing a variety of verses, such as
the ones listed here, the potential for fostering mutual learning
and development is created in the context of an engaging interactive communication process. Such a discussion, anchored to
Jesus' teachings, should enable participants to discover a better sense of what being a servant leader might mean for themselves and others.

Suggested Discussion Questions

My own experience has been that often the key can be to have
some good overall questions that effectively engage both the
thinking and participation of group members. The following
list of potential discussion questions is intended only as a starting point for generating questions that fit the needs of your
specific group. I encourage you to consider each question and
whether it would be a helpful point of departure for dialogue.
I also encourage you to adapt and rewrite the questions as you
see fit and to generate your own questions that are customized
to your unique context.

1. Why are Jesus' teachings relevant for organizations today?
   Why should we look to Jesus' teachings for leadership
   guidance?

2. What are some of the major points you feel Jesus was trying to make that are relevant to leadership today?

3. What does the wisdom of Jesus suggest is the first thing
   people should do if they want to become effective
   leaders?

4. Do you believe that you need to be a Christian to benefit
   from Jesus' teachings for leadership? In what ways might

Jesus' teachings guide leaders associated with various religions and cultures to help make the world a more caring and healthier place for us all?

5. Are there organizations that you feel exemplify the spirit of Jesus' teachings? Can you provide concrete examples?

6. Are there leaders that you feel exemplify the spirit of Jesus' teachings? Can you provide concrete examples?

7. What about your organization/place of work? Does it operate in a way that is consistent with the wisdom of Jesus? What parts of the organization and what people do you believe act according to Jesus' teachings? What kind of results do they reap from what they sow?

8. What are the risks of adopting principles consistent with the teachings of Jesus in your work and leadership?

9. What are some potential benefits of adopting behavior consistent with the wisdom of Jesus in your life? In your career?

10. Discuss the following ideas. How could you more fully put them into practice in your own behavior and leadership, and what would be the likely results?

- Lead yourself first
- The Golden Rule
- Servant Leadership
- Compassion
- Forgiveness
- Humility

- Gathering all the "lost sheep"
- Recognizing the value of every person
- Planting golden mustard seeds

11. What other issues do you believe are important considerations in trying to act consistently with the teachings of Jesus in your life, work, and leadership?

12. What other questions related to the book might be especially pertinent to your group?

In addition to the general discussion questions offered above, more specific questions can be developed depending on the type of discussion group it is. The following sample questions are intended to be only a starting point for group discussion in categories of groups including those consisting of business colleagues, educational groups, church groups, and community groups. I suggest looking to these questions as an initial source of inspiration and then generating other questions that are more targeted and customized to your specific group.

1. **For a Business Group.** Is it appropriate for a profit-based business to practice the kind of compassion, forgiveness, and integrity that Jesus taught? Is prioritizing ends such as social benefit for people in need or protection of the natural environment, rather than return on investment, something that should be reserved for nonprofit organizations? Is it realistic to expect a business that is committed first and foremost to serving the wellbeing of its employees, customers, and society in general, as well as the health of the planet, to be able to compete in a highly competitive business world?

2. **For an Educational Group.** Does *The Leadership Wisdom of Jesus* have a legitimate place in educational settings such as a college classroom or a professional training program? Are the lessons Jesus taught two thousand years ago still a credible source of practical guidance today for life and work, let alone for wisdom? Why or why not? What can be learned from the methods Jesus used to teach others and the kind of learning it facilitated?

3. **For a Church Group.** Does the church and its members operate and behave in accordance with *The Leadership Wisdom of Jesus?* To what extent do church politics interfere with realizing this ideal? Does church bureaucracy hinder the church from acting in ways that Jesus taught that people should serve and behave toward one another? Is the style and behavior of the church leadership consistent with *The Leadership Wisdom of Jesus?* To what extent are all members of the church invited and allowed to participate in leading themselves and others?

4. **For a Community Group.** Do the members of the community practice the kind of behavior toward one another that Jesus taught? What kind of leadership is practiced in our community? Is it consistent with *The Leadership Wisdom of Jesus?* Is our community a caring and supportive place to live? How could it become more so than it is? What kind of leadership does our community encourage and allow from its members? Is it consistent with what Jesus taught?

I hope the suggestions and questions offered in this discussion guide are helpful to you for creating a highly engaging and insightful reading and discussion group or class. One of the interesting aspects of Jesus' teaching style is that he often shared examples and stories that allowed others to interpret meaning and relevance to their own situation. Rather than taking a condescending stance, he solicited the thinking and participation of the listener. It seems appropriate that a discussion group or class addressing the material presented in this book, which was written with the hope of effectively drawing on the wisdom Jesus shared, would similarly draw people in to think for themselves. As Jesus effectively demonstrated, this kind of highly involving approach can be a potent way to consider and discuss the meaning of some very powerful ideas that are capable of changing the way we think about life, work, and leadership forever. I sincerely hope that this short guide and the content of this book will help you and your group to capture this kind of spirit.

Notes

INTRODUCTION

1. See, for example, Robert W. Funk, Roy W. Hoover, and The Jesus Seminar, *The Five Gospels* (New York: Macmillan, 1994).

PART ONE: CLEAN THE MIRROR IMAGE

LOGS BEFORE SPECKS, OR LEAD THYSELF FIRST

1. The New Revised Standard Version of the Bible is the primary source of scripture passages throughout this book.

THE LAST SHALL BE FIRST

1. James B. Treece, "How Ford Did It," *Business Week*, Oct. 14, 1991, p. 26; and Donald E. Petersen and John Hillkirk, *A Better Idea: Redefining the Way Americans Work* (New York: Houghton Mifflin, 1991).
2. "A Better Idea? Ford's Leaders Push Radical Shift in Culture as Competition Grows," *The Wall Street Journal*, Dec. 3, 1985.
3. "Ford's Idea Machine—A Once-Troubled Giant Discovers a Recipe for Recovery: Change Everything," *Newsweek*, Nov. 24, 1986, p. 66.
4. "Fortune 500/CNN Moneyline Poll: The No. 1 Leader Is Petersen of Ford," *Fortune*, Oct. 24, 1988, pp. 69–70.
5. See "The 'tipping point' in Ford's turnaround" by Patricia Sellers, CNNMoney.com, December 20, 2010.
6. Joe DeMatio, "2010 Man of the Year: Alan Mulally, CEO Ford Motor Company," *Automobile Magazine*, November, 2009.

STOP WORRYING

1. See Leonard Sweet, The Jesus Prescription for a Healthy Life (Nashville: Abingdon Press, 1996).
2. See for example, Kathi Lovelace, Charles C. Manz, and Jose Alves, "Work Stress and Leadership Development: The Role of Self-Leadership, Shared Leadership, Physical Fitness and Flow in Managing Demands and Increasing Job Control," Human Resource Management Review, 2007,17, pp 374-387.
3. See Julie Amparano, "Workers Fear Job Loss," Arizona Republic, Jan. 29, 1997, pp. E1, E3.
4. James Lincoln Collier, "Winning over Worry," Reader's Digest, Apr. 1988, pp. 183–186.
5. Collier, "Winning over Worry," p. 186.

COMMIT TO ETHICAL BEHAVIOR

1. See Charles C. Manz and Henry P. Sims, Jr., The New SuperLeadership: Leading Others to Lead Themselves (San Francisco: Berrett-Koehler, 2001).
2. See Kenneth R. Andrews, Ethics in Practice: Managing the Moral Corporation (Boston: Harvard Business School Press, 1989), p. 281.
3. See Sherry Boas, "Generation X's Values Revealed in ASU Class," Tempe Tribune, Feb. 10, 1997, pp. A1, A6.
4. Keshavan Nair, A Higher Standard of Leadership: Lessons from the Life of Gandhi (San Francisco: Berrett-Koehler, 1994), p. 52.
5. Nair, A Higher Standard of Leadership, p. 52.
6. Boas, "Generation X's Values . . . ," p. A6.

LET YOUR LIGHT SHINE

1. This account of the leadership of Dean Cycon and the business approach of Dean's Beans is based on an ongoing study of the company as of 2011 (by the author along with co-investigators Robert Marx and Karen Manz) involving interviews, direct observations, review of company documents and the company's web site, and other published materials.
2. Ricardo Semler, "Managing Without Managers," Harvard Business Review, Sept.–Oct. 1989, pp. 76–84.

3. Semler, "Managing Without Managers," p. 84.

4. Frank O'Donnell, "When Workers Are Bosses," *The Washington Post,* Sept. 14, 1993, p. B-2.

PART TWO: LEAD OTHERS WITH COMPASSION

LOVE YOUR FRIENDS AND YOUR ENEMIES

1. For a more detailed account of this case see Charles C. Manz, David E. Keating, and Anne Donnellon, "Preparing for an Organizational Change to Employee Self-Management: The Managerial Transition," *Organizational Dynamics,* 1990, *19,* pp. 15–26.

THE GOLDEN RULE AND BEYOND

1. Robert Rosenthal and Lenore Jacobson, *Pygmalion in the Classroom: Teacher Expectations and Pupils' Intellectual Development* (New York: Holt, Rinehart and Winston, 1968).

PUT THE GAVEL AWAY

1. For more information on this case see Meg Cox and Johnie L. Roberts, "How the Despotic Boss of Simon & Schuster Found Himself Jobless," *The Wall Street Journal,* July 6, 1994, pp. A7, A9; Michael Meyer and Nancy Hass, "Simon Says 'Out!'" *Newsweek,* June 27, 1994, pp. 42–44; and Henry P. Sims, Jr. and Charles C. Manz, *Company of Heroes* (New York: Wiley, 1996), p. 27.

2. Jon Kabat-Zinn, *Wherever You Go, There You Are: Mindfulness Meditation in Everyday Life* (New York: Hyperion, 1994), p. 3.

GATHER THE LOST SHEEP

1. See, for example, Charles C. Manz and Henry P. Sims, Jr., *Business Without Bosses: How Self-Managing Teams Are Building High-Performing Companies* (New York: Wiley, 1993).

2. See Kenneth Smith and Henry P. Sims, Jr., "The Strategy Team: Teams at the Top," in Charles C. Manz and Henry P. Sims, Jr., *Business Without Bosses* (New York: Wiley, 1993).

PART THREE: LEAD OTHERS TO BE THEIR BEST SELVES

PREPARE THE SOIL

1. See Kurt Lewin, *Field Theory in Social Science* (New York: HarperCollins, 1951) and Kurt Lewin, "Frontiers in Group Dynamics," *Human Relations,* 1947, *1,* pp. 5–41.
2. For a more detailed description of this case see Henry P. Sims, Jr., Charles C. Manz, and Barry Bateman, "The Early Implementation Phase: Getting Teams Started in the Office," in Charles C. Manz and Henry P. Sims, Jr., *Business Without Bosses* (New York: Wiley, 1993), pp. 85–114.

BE FORGIVING—ALLOW MISTAKES
FOR THE SAKE OF LEARNING

1. I am not aware of a published source for this story, which I learned about through word of mouth. One of the reviewers of an earlier draft of this book had also heard the story and indicated that his sources identified IBM as the company involved.
2. Henri J. M. Nouwen, *The Return of the Prodigal Son: A Story of Homecoming* (New York: Image Books, 1992).

LEAD BY SERVING

1. This example is adapted from an information email sent out by Judi Neal on behalf of the Association For Spirit at Work (ASAW) on January 17, 2005.
2. See Robert K. Greenleaf, *On Becoming a Servant-Leader* (San Francisco: Jossey-Bass, 1997), *Seeker and Servant* (San Francisco: Jossey-Bass, 1997), *and The Leader as Servant* (Newton Center, Mass.: The Robert K. Greenleaf Center, 1970).
3. Greenleaf, *The Leader as Servant,* p. 4.
4. Greenleaf, *The Leader as Servant,* p. 7.
5. For more Information on the service oriented management practices at Herman Miller see Charles C. Manz, Karen P. Manz, Stephen B. Adams, and Frank Shipper (Forthcoming) "Sustainable Performance With Values-Based Shared Leadership: A Case Study of a Virtuous Organization," *Canadian Journal of Administrative Sciences.*

6. Charles C. Manz, Craig L. Pearce & Henry P. Sims, Jr. "Special Issue: The Ins and Outs of Leading Teams," *Organizational Dynamics*, Volume 38, July-September, 2009.

7. Craig L. Pearce, Charles C. Manz & Henry P. Sims, Jr. "Where Do We Go From Here: Is Shared Leadership the Key to Team Success?," *Organizational Dynamics*, Volume 38, July-September, 2009, pp. 234-238.

8. Charles C. Manz and John Newstrom, "The Good and the Bad of Teams: A Practical Look at Successes and Challenges," in Charles C. Manz and Henry P. Sims, Jr., *Business Without Bosses* (New York: Wiley, 1993), pp. 65–83.

9. Henry P. Sims, Jr., Charles C. Manz, and Barry Bateman, "The Early Implementation Phase: Getting Teams Started in the Office," in Charles C. Manz and Henry P. Sims, Jr., *Business Without Bosses* (New York: Wiley, 1993), pp. 102–103.

10. Manz and Sims, *Business Without Bosses*, p. 75.

11. Manz and Sims, *Business Without Bosses*, p. 103.

LEAD WITHOUT BLINDNESS

1. See Bernard Bass, *Bass and Stogdill's Handbook of Leadership* (New York: Free Press, 1990). Also, for a more recent update of this Handbook, see Bernard M. Bass and Ruth Bass *The Bass Handbook of Leadership: Theory, Research, and Managerial Applications* (New York: Free Press, 2009).

2. See Christopher P. Neck and Charles C. Manz, *Mastering Self-Leadership: Empowering Yourself for Personal Excellence*, 5th Edition, (Upper Saddle River, New Jersey: Prentice-Hall, 2010).

THE VALUE OF PENNIES

1. A primary source for this short account of the life of Rudy Ruettiger was Christopher P. Neck, "Rudy! Rudy! Rudy! Dreams Do Come True," in Henry P. Sims, Jr. and Charles C. Manz, *Company of Heroes: Unleashing the Power of Self-Leadership* (New York: Wiley, 1996).

INSTILL COMMITMENT, NOT GREED

1. See, for example, B. F. Skinner, *Beyond Freedom and Dignity* (New York: Knopf, 1971).

2. See, for example, J. Adams, "Toward an Understanding of Inequity," *Journal of Abnormal and Social Psychology,* 1963, 67, pp. 422–436.

3. See Frank Shipper and Charles C. Manz, "Self-Management Without Formal Teams: The Organization as Team," in Charles C. Manz and Henry P. Sims, Jr., *Business Without Bosses* (New York: Wiley, 1993), p. 134. Also, for a more recent article reporting on Gore's distinctive approach to leading and organizing see Charles C., Manz, Frank Shipper and Greg L. Stewart, "Everyone a Team Leader: Do the Shared Leadership Practices of W. L. Gore Provide an Answer to the Question 'Where Do We Go From Here?'," *Organizational Dynamics,* Volume 38, July–September, 2009, pp. 239–244.

4. This information on Equal Exchange is based on an ongoing study of the company as of 2011 (by the author along with co-investigators Frank Shipper, Benita Harris, and Karen Manz) involving interviews, direct observations, review of company documents and the company's web site, and other published materials. For more Information on Equal Exchange's democratic coop organizational design and approach visit www.equalexchange.coop/worker-owned.

PART FOUR: PLANT GOLDEN MUSTARD SEEDS

PRACTICE MUSTARD SEED POWER

1. See *Random Acts of Kindness* and the follow-up books *More Random Acts of Kindness* and *Kids' Random Acts of Kindness* (Berkeley, Calif.: Conari, 1993).

2. For a more detailed discussion of strongman and visionary hero leadership, see Henry P. Sims, Jr. and Charles C. Manz, *Company of Heroes: Unleashing the Power of Self-Leadership* (New York: Wiley, 1996) and *The New SuperLeadership: Leading Others to Lead Themselves* by Charles C. Manz and Henry P. Sims, Jr. (San Francisco: Berrett-Koehler, 2001).

LEAD WITH THE POWER OF GOLDEN MUSTARD SEEDS

1. This example is based on the leadership profile titled "Carly Fiorina of Hewlett-Packard" by Seokhwa Yun and Henry P. Sims, Jr. appearing in the book *The New SuperLeadership: Leading Others to Lead Themselves* by Charles C. Manz and Henry P. Sims, Jr. (San Francisco: Berrett-Koehler, 2001), pp. 87–93.
2. *Ibid*, pp. 88–89.
3. *Ibid*, p. 93.
4. This account of Aaron Feuerstein's leadership at Malden Mills is based on Julie Amparano, "Taking Good Care of Workers Pays Off," *The Arizona Republic*, Jan. 23, 1997, pp. E1, E8.
5. This information is based in part on the more detailed account of the continued story of Malden Mills and its CEO Aaron Feuerstein titled "Malden Mills: A Contemporary Story of Spiritual and Business Wisdom" by Robert D. Marx, appearing in the essay "Spiritual Beliefs and Scholarship" by Charles C. Manz, Karen P. Manz, Robert D. Marx, and Christopher P. Neck, *Management Communications Quarterly*, Vol. 17, May 2004, pp. 611–620.

DON'T TRY TO SERVE TWO MASTERS

1. This example is based on information in the December 23, 2004 article "Face Time With Meg Whitman," *Fast Company*, located online at http://pf.fastcompany.com/magazine/46/facetime.html.
2. Walsh, J.P., K. Weber, and J.D. Margolis, (2003) "Social issues in management: Our lost cause found." Journal of Management, 29: pp. 859–881
3. "First, Walk the Course," as told to Eve Tahmincioglu, New York Times, BU, p. 9, January 30, 2005.
4. For more on the role of virtues in organizations see the edited book Charles C. Manz, Kim S. Cameron, Karen P.Manz, and Robert D. Marx (Eds.), *The Virtuous Organization: Insights From Some of the World's Leading Management Thinkers* (Singapore: World Scientific Publishers, 2008).

INDEX

accountability, overemphasis on,
53–54
AES Corporation, 84–85
American Express
change process at, 91
team leadership in, 107
worker empowerment and, 83
Andrews, Kenneth, 39
aphorisms, Jesus' use of, 3
Aristotle
on greatest good, 99
Association for Spirit at Work, 103
AT&T, 83

Bakke, Dennis, 84, 85
Banister, Roger, 139
belief, power of, 139–145
Biondi, Frank, Jr., 74
blindness, leading without, 111–115
Boeing, Inc., 19, 83
Buddha, 1, 65

carrot-and-stick approach, 124,
125
Caterpillar, 83
change, groundwork for, 89–94
children, emulating, 16–17, 21,
103
Chrysler, 19, 75
cleansing insides, 23–27
commitment, instilling, 123–130
compassion vs. self-righteousness,
52–53
concrete payoffs, 99–100
Confucius, 1, 65
contributions, value of, 117–121

Cummins Engine, 83
Cycon, Dean, 45–46, 149

Dean's Beans, 45–46, 149
defilement, 23, 27
De Pree, D. J., 105
De Pree, Max, 105
Digital Equipment, 83
discussion guide, 167–178
Disney, 149
distractions, 93
dressing for success, 23

eBay, 149
Edison, Thomas, 139
empathy, 65–69
empowerment, 52, 113
enemies, love for, 57–63
Enron, 24, 148
Equal Exchange, 127–128
equity theory, 124–125
ethical behavior, committing to,
37–42
*Ethics in Practice: Managing the
Moral Corporation* (Andrews),
39
expendability, lack of, 79–85

failure
compassion in face of, 53
as learning experience, 54–55
fairness, 84
Fair Trade, 45
faith, power of, 139–145
Feuerstein, Aaron, 41, 142–143,
145, 148–149

ABOUT THE AUTHOR

Charles C. Manz, PhD, is a speaker, consultant, and bestselling business author. He holds the Charles and Janet Nirenberg Chair of Leadership in the Isenberg School of Management at the University of Massachusetts. His work has been featured on radio and television and in *The Wall Street Journal, Fortune, U.S. News & World Report, Success, Psychology Today, Fast Company* and several other national publications. He received the prestigious Marvin Bower Fellow-ship at the Harvard Business School which is "awarded for outstanding achievement in research and productivity, influence, and leadership in business scholarship." He earned a PhD in Business, with an emphasis in Organizational Behavior and Psychology, from The Pennsylvania State University and MBA and BA degrees from Michigan State University.

He is the author or co-author of over 200 articles and scholarly papers and more than 20 books including the bestsellers *Business Without Bosses: How Self-Managing Teams Are Building High-Performing Companies,* the Stybel-Peabody prize-winning *SuperLeadership: Leading Others to Lead Themselves, Mastering Self-Leadership: Empowering Yourself for Personal Excellence, The Power of Failure: 27 Ways to Turn Life's Setbacks Into Success,* and *The Leadership Wisdom of Jesus: Practical Lessons For Today.* Other books by Dr. Manz include *Foreword Magazine* best-book-of-the-year Gold Award winner in the self-help category *Emotional Discipline: The Power to Choose How You Feel; The New Super-Leadership: Leading Others to Lead Themselves; The Greatest Leader Who Wasn't: A Leadership Fable; Fit to Lead: The Proven 8-Week Solution for Shaping Up Your Body, Your Mind, and Your Career; The Power to Choose How You Feel* (short booklet format); *Temporary Sanity: Instant Self-Leadership Strategies for Turbulent Times; The Wisdom of Solomon at Work: Ancient Virtues for Living and Leading Today; Company of Heroes: Unleashing the Power of Self-Leadership; For Team Members Only: Making Your Workplace Team Productive and Hassle-Free;* and *Teamwork and Group Dynamics.* Some of his newest books are *The Virtuous Organization: Insights From Some of the World's Leading Management Thinkers, Nice Guys Can Get the Corner Office: Eight Strategies for Winning in Business Without Being a Jerk,* a new fifth edition of *Mastering Self-Leadership;* and his forthcoming co-authored book *Share the Lead.* His books have been translated into many languages, and featured in book clubs, and on audio tape and CD.

Dr. Manz has served as a consultant for many organizations, including 3M, Ford, Motorola, Xerox, the Mayo Clinic, Procter & Gamble, General Motors, American Express, Allied Signal, Unisys, Josten's Learning, Banc One, the American Hospital Association, the American College of Physician Executives, the U.S. and Canadian governments, and many others.

Charles C. Manz, Karen P. Manz,
Robert D. Marx, and Christopher P. Neck

The Wisdom of Solomon at Work
Ancient Virtues for Living and Leading Today

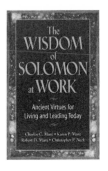

The Wisdom of Solomon at Work illuminates the abiding virtues—faith, courage, compassion, integrity, and justice—that equip us to meet life's challenges. Using personal stories to show how people today are reconciling spiritual values with the pressures of modern life, the authors provide a fresh, contemporary perspective on the timeless wisdom of the Old Testament.

Hardcover, 192 pages, ISBN 978-1-57675-085-8
PDF ebook, ISBN 978-1-60994-163-5

Charles C. Manz

The Power of Failure
27 Ways to Turn Life's Setbacks into Success

The fear of failure is enough to stop many people in their tracks, but Charles Manz shows that failure is an essential component of personal and professional success. Using real-life examples and stories, Manz shows that challenges are disguised opportunities, competition spurs positive change, setbacks catalyze creative coping skills, and "collaboration" with failure can be an ongoing part of being successful.

Paperback, 168 pages, ISBN 978-1-57675-132-9
PDF ebook, ISBN 978-1-60509-389-5

BK Berrett–Koehler Publishers, Inc.
www.bkconnection.com   1 800 929 2929

Charles C. Manz

Emotional Discipline
The Power to Choose How You Feel

Emotional Discipline details five easy-to-learn steps and twenty-five specific strategies for responding to your feelings in the present and preparing for emotional challenges in the future. This remarkable approach combines mind, body, and spirit to help you deal with arguably the most challenging part of the human condition: the constant fluctuations in how you feel that color your experience of life and limit your personal effectiveness.

Paperback, 256 pages, ISBN 978-1-57675-230-2
PDF ebook, ISBN 978-1-57675-962-2

Charles C. Manz and Henry P. Sims, Jr.

The New SuperLeadership
Leading Others to Lead Themselves

Drawing on contemporary examples, many from the high-tech and information sectors, Manz and Sims show that the best leaders move ahead while maximizing the contributions of others. This practical guide will teach you how to be a SuperLeader by turning followers into extraordinary self-leaders—pillars of strength that will support the organization at every level.

Hardcover, 272 pages, ISBN 978-1-57675-105-3
PDF ebook, ISBN 978-1-60509-715-2

BK® Berrett–Koehler Publishers, Inc.
www.bkconnection.com   1 800 929 2929

Berrett–Koehler
Publishers

Berrett-Koehler is an independent publisher dedicated to an ambitious mission: *Creating a World That Works for All*.

We believe that to truly create a better world, action is needed at all levels—individual, organizational, and societal. At the individual level, our publications help people align their lives with their values and with their aspirations for a better world. At the organizational level, our publications promote progressive leadership and management practices, socially responsible approaches to business, and humane and effective organizations. At the societal level, our publications advance social and economic justice, shared prosperity, sustainability, and new solutions to national and global issues.

A major theme of our publications is "Opening Up New Space." Berrett-Koehler titles challenge conventional thinking, introduce new ideas, and foster positive change. Their common quest is changing the underlying beliefs, mindsets, institutions, and structures that keep generating the same cycles of problems, no matter who our leaders are or what improvement programs we adopt.

We strive to practice what we preach—to operate our publishing company in line with the ideas in our books. At the core of our approach is stewardship, which we define as a deep sense of responsibility to administer the company for the benefit of all of our "stakeholder" groups: authors, customers, employees, investors, service providers, and the communities and environment around us.

We are grateful to the thousands of readers, authors, and other friends of the company who consider themselves to be part of the "BK Community." We hope that you, too, will join us in our mission.

A BK Business Book

This book is part of our BK Business series. BK Business titles pioneer new and progressive leadership and management practices in all types of public, private, and nonprofit organizations. They promote socially responsible approaches to business, innovative organizational change methods, and more humane and effective organizations.

Berrett–Koehler
Publishers

A community dedicated to creating
a world that works for all

Visit Our Website: www.bkconnection.com

Read book excerpts, see author videos and Internet movies, read
our authors' blogs, join discussion groups, download book apps, find
out about the BK Affiliate Network, browse subject-area libraries of
books, get special discounts, and more!

Subscribe to Our Free E-Newsletter, the *BK Communiqué*

Be the first to hear about new publications, special discount offers,
exclusive articles, news about bestsellers, and more! Get on the list
for our free e-newsletter by going to **www.bkconnection.com**.

Get Quantity Discounts

Berrett-Koehler books are available at quantity discounts for orders
of ten or more copies. Please call us toll-free at (800) 929-2929 or
email us at bkp.orders@aidcvt.com.

Join the BK Community

BKcommunity.com is a virtual meeting place where people from
around the world can engage with kindred spirits to create a world
that works for all. BKcommunity.com members may create their own
profiles, blog, start and participate in forums and discussion groups,
post photos and videos, answer surveys, announce and register for
upcoming events, and chat with others online in real time. Please join
the conversation!